THE ROAD TO APPOMATTOX

A SOURCEBOOK ON THE CIVIL WAR

THE ROAD TO APPOMATTOX

A SOURCEBOOK ON THE CIVIL WAR

Edited by Carter Smith

AMERICAN ALBUMS FROM THE COLLECTIONS OF

THE LIBRARY OF CONGRESS

THE MILLBROOK PRESS, *Brookfield, Connecticut*

Cover: "Sheridan's Ride." Lithograph by L. Prang & Co., 1864.

Title Page: "Going into Camp at Night." Oil painting by Edwin Forbes, 1876.

Contents Page: "The Two Standard Bearers, the Day After Battle."

Back Cover: "Battle of Mobile Bay." Lithograph by L. Prang & Co., after J. O. Davidson, 1886.

Library of Congress Cataloging-in-Publication Data

The road to Appomattox : a sourcebook on the Civil War / edited by Carter Smith.
     p. cm. — (American albums from the collections of the Library of Congress)
    Includes bibliographical references and index.
    Summary: Uses a variety of contemporary materials to describe and illustrate the battles fought between January 1864 and April 1865 that led to the end of the Civil War.
    ISBN 1-56294-264-6 (lib. bdg.) ISBN 1-56294-881-4 (pbk.)
    1. United States—History—Civil War, 1861–1865—Campaigns—Juvenile literature. 2. United States—History—Civil War, 1861–1865—Campaigns—Pictorial works—Juvenile literature. 3. United States—History—Civil War, 1861–1865—Campaigns—Sources—Juvenile literature. 4. Appomattox Campaign, 1865—Juvenile literature. 5. Appomattox Campaign, 1865—Pictorial works—Juvenile literature. 6. Appomattox Campaign, 1865—Sources—Juvenile literature. [1. United States—History—Civil War, 1861–1865—Campaigns—Sources. 2. Appomattox Campaign, 1865—Sources.]
I. Smith, C. Carter. II. Series.
E470.R63 1993
973.7'36'0222—dc20
                              92-16546
                                  CIP
                                  AC

 Created in association with Media Projects Incorporated

C. Carter Smith, *Executive Editor*
Lelia Wardwell, *Managing Editor*
Charles A. Wills, *Principal Writer*
Kimberly Horstman, *Picture and Production Editor*
Lydia Link, *Designer*
Athena Angelos, *Photo Researcher*

The consultation of Bernard F. Reilly, Jr., Head Curator of the Prints and Photographs Division of the Library of Congress, is gratefully acknowledged.

Contents

Introduction   7

A Timeline of Major Events   10

Part I
Total War   17

Part II
Nearing the End   53

Resource Guide   94

Index   95

Despite the Civil War, the Union managed to hold a presidential election in 1864. To win support from pro-war Democrats, the Republican Party temporarily renamed itself the Union Party, and Andrew Johnson—a Democrat and the military governor of Tennessee—joined the ticket as Abraham Lincoln's running mate.

Introduction

THE ROAD TO APPOMATTOX is one of the volumes in a series published by The Millbrook Press titled AMERICAN ALBUMS FROM THE COLLECTIONS OF THE LIBRARY OF CONGRESS, and one of six books in the series subtitled SOURCEBOOKS ON THE CIVIL WAR.

The editors' basic goal for the series is to make available to the student many of the original visual documents preserved in the Library of Congress as records of the American past. The volumes in THE CIVIL WAR series reproduce prints, maps, paintings, and other works in the Library's special collections divisions, and a few from its general book collections. Most prominently featured in this series are the holdings of the Prints and Photographs Division.

Many of the images presented in this volume are the field drawings produced by artists like A. R. Waud, Edwin Forbes, and others—men who followed the Army of the Potomac and the Union fleets throughout the war, recording in ink and pencil the events and people that shaped the course of the war. Near the end of the war, one can read in these drawings the disorder and exhaustion that marked this stage in the conflict. The viewer notes such tangible signs of the army's deteriorating means as Waud's reliance on any small or rough scrap of paper for his sketches. The desperate turn of the initially glorious Northern military enterprise is apparent also in the photographic records, where officers who projected confident, even gallant, demeanors on portraits taken earlier in the war now turn disinterestedly toward—or even away from—the camera.

The toll taken on the South is also apparent in the images from the war. George Barnard's photographic record of the Sherman campaign through Georgia and South Carolina is one of the most extraordinary achievements in the history of war photography. Barnard's photographs are poignant, almost mournful, in their dry detailing of the ruin that Sherman's army left in its wake. The first Northern photographs of the fallen Richmond show a city equally devastated.

Many of the paintings used in this volume, on the other hand, were reproduced from chromolithographs made in the 1880s and 1890s, long after the war had ended. They add dignity and a sense of order to battle that was easier to supply in retrospect than in the heat of events.

The documents reproduced here represent a small but telling portion of the rich pictorial record of the Civil War preserved by the Library of Congress in its role as the nation's library.

BERNARD F. REILLY, JR.

By the summer of 1861, the Confederacy consisted of eleven states, and its territory stretched from the Atlantic Coast into the Trans-Mississippi West. By the end of 1864, the Confederacy was reduced to Virginia, North and South Carolina, and isolated pockets in the West, and was involved in an almost entirely defensive war. The following sixteen months would see Union forces occupying more and more Southern territory as simultaneous offensives pushed the dwindling Southern armies back. In the spring of 1864, Ulysses S. Grant launched a major offensive in Virginia, while William Tecumseh Sherman and his army moved into Georgia.

As Sherman and Grant pressed the Confederacy on land, the Union naval blockade continued to tighten along the Southern coast. Both Mobile, Alabama, and Savannah, Georgia, were captured by Union forces, and as 1865 began, only one major port—Wilmington, North Carolina—was left in Confederate hands. On January 15, 1865, it too was closed by a Union amphibious force.

The Confederacy shrank further during Sherman's march through the Carolinas in February–March 1865. In April, Grant's final offensive in Virginia ended with the fall of Richmond and the surrender of the Army of Northern Virginia. Southern forces still controlled some territory in the West, but by the end of May 1865 the United States was again under one flag.

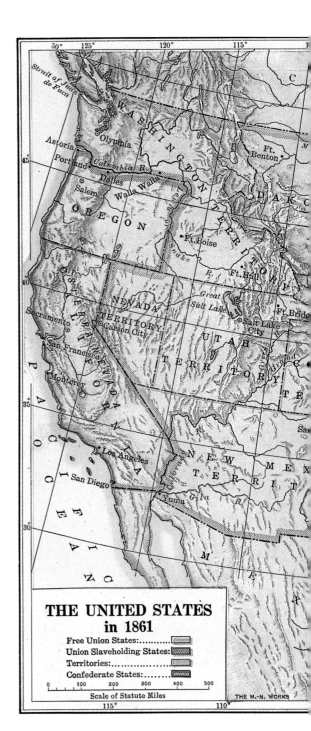

THE UNITED STATES in 1861

Free Union States:...........⬚
Union Slaveholding States:▨
Territories:.................⬚
Confederate States:........▨

Scale of Statute Miles

0   100   200   300   400   500

THE M.-N. WORKS

A TIMELINE OF MAJOR EVENTS
January 1864–June 1864

AT HOME AND ABROAD

January 4, 1864 Confederate president Jefferson Davis orders General Robert E. Lee to take food from farms to feed his troops.

February 17 President Davis suspends habeas corpus in the Confederacy, although only for arrests authorized by the secretary of war or Davis himself. Vice President Alexander Stephens opposes the action.

March 5 The Confederate Congress orders that all ships entering Confederate ports must devote at least half their cargo space to supplies needed by the Confederate government.

April 7 The U.S. Senate passes the Thirteenth Amendment to the Constitution. Once approved by the House and ratified by the states, the amendment

Celebrating the passage of the Thirteenth Amendment

will permanently abolish slavery in the United States.

April 10 Napoleon III of France declares the Archduke Maximilian emperor of

Mexico. The move clearly violates the Monroe Doctrine, but Washington is too busy fighting the Confederacy to oppose it.

MILITARY EVENTS

March 8, 1864 President Lincoln appoints General Ulysses S. Grant commander of the Union Army; ten days later, General William Sherman

General William T. Sherman

takes overall command of Union forces in the Western Theater.

March 15 The Red River Campaign opens in Louisiana; Union forces under General Nathaniel Banks move into western Louisiana and eastern Texas to keep the cotton-rich area from the Confederacy. The campaign eventually fails.

April 12 Confederate general Nathan

Bedford Forrest captures Fort Pillow, Kentucky. Over 230 of the Union defenders, mostly black soldiers, are killed by Forrest's troops after the fort surrenders.

May 5 Grant and Lee's armies battle in dense woods in Virginia called the Wilderness.

May 6 Confederate general James Longstreet is seriously wounded in the Battle of the Wilderness.

May 8 The Confederate and Union armies clash again near Spotsylvania, Virginia, in the opening skirmishes of what will become a four-day battle.

May 12 After days of fruitless fighting at Spotsylvania, Grant orders a frontal assault on well-entrenched Confederate positions.

May 11 A cavalry raid by Union general Philip Sheridan is temporarily halted at

May 4 The U.S. House of Representatives passes the Wade-Davis Reconstruction Bill. The law—supported by Congress's Radical Republicans—would impose harsh penalties on the South if a Union victory is achieved.

May 31 Republicans opposed to Lincoln nominate General John C. Frémont for president at their convention in Cleveland, Ohio.

June The U.S. Senate refuses to seat members from Arkansas, Tennessee, and Louisiana, who are seeking entrance under the Lincoln Reconstruction Plan.

June 7–8 The National Union

A Lincoln/Johnson campaign poster

Convention meets in Baltimore, Maryland, and nominates Lincoln for reelection; Lincoln chooses Governor Andrew Johnson of Tennessee as his running mate.

June 30 Secretary of the Treasury Salmon Chase offers his resignation to Lincoln for a third time, and it is accepted. Chase is replaced by William Fessenden.

Yellow Tavern, Virginia, but Confederate general J.E.B. Stuart is killed in the battle.

May 13 Sheridan destroys Lee's supply depots at Hanover Junction and Beaver Dam, Virginia.

May 15 Union troops in Virginia's Shenandoah Valley suffer a defeat at New Market, in the Western Theater.

June 1 Grant's army moves toward the town of Cold

Harbor, Virginia, where several important supply roads join. Lee moves into position to meet him.

June 2–3 Grant orders charge after charge on the Confederate positions at the Battle of Cold Harbor; none succeed. Losses are enormous, with Grant's army suffering heavier casualties than Lee's.

June 15–18 The Union Army moves into Petersburg, Virginia, but fails

to capture the city. Grant finally orders his troops to dig in and prepare for a siege.

June 19 The USS *Kearsarge* sinks the Confederate warship *Alabama* in the English Channel near Cherbourg, France, ending the *Alabama*'s career as the South's most effective commerce raider.

June 23 In an effort to draw troops away from Petersburg, Confederate

general Jubal Early leads a cavalry force up the Shenandoah Valley toward Washington.

June 27 Sherman's troops make three unsuccessful attempts to drive General Joseph E. Johnston's Confederates from their positions in the Battle of Kenesaw Mountain, Georgia.

A TIMELINE OF MAJOR EVENTS
July 1864–December 1864

AT HOME AND ABROAD

July 4, 1864 President Lincoln vetoes the Wade-Davis Reconstruction Bill; he makes it known that he favors a kinder postwar policy toward the South.

August 30 Democratic Party leaders declare the four-year Union war effort to be a failure and add a "peace plank" to their platform—a call for an immediate end to the war.

August 31 George McClellan, former commander of the Army of the Potomac, and George Pendleton are nominated as the Democratic choice for president and vice president.

September 3 Lincoln declares a day of celebration in the North to commemorate the victories at Atlanta and Mobile Bay.

September 8 McClellan accepts

Atlanta in ruins

the Democratic presidential nomination, but rejects the party platform's "peace plank."

September 17 John C. Frémont withdraws from the

presidential race and lends his support to Lincoln.

October 31 Nevada is admitted to the Union as the 36th state.

MILITARY EVENTS

July 11–12, 1864 Jubal Early's raiders attack Fort Stevens, on the outskirts of Washington. President Lincoln watches the assault.

July 17 Sherman's army finally arrives outside of Atlanta, Georgia, after a two-month-long march. The city is defended by Confederate general John Bell Hood.

July 22 Hood's forces attack

Sherman along Peachtree Creek, but fail to drive off the Union troops.

July 30 Union engineers explode a huge mine under the Confederate trenches outside Petersburg, Virginia. The explosion blows a hole in the Confederate lines, but a follow-up attack by Union infantrymen fails.

August 1 Union general Philip

Sheridan moves into the Shenandoah Valley to drive Jubal Early's Confederates from the rich (and strategically important) region.

August 5 A Union fleet under Admiral David Farragut succeeds in capturing Mobile, Alabama, an important Confederate port, in the Battle of Mobile Bay.

August 31 A last-ditch attempt to keep Sherman's army out of Atlanta

ends with a Confederate defeat at Jonesboro, Georgia. Hood's army abandons the city on September 1; Sherman enters the city the next day.

September 19 A small band of Confederates crosses the Canadian border and attempts to seize a Union gunboat on Lake Erie and free Confederate prisoners from Johnson's Island. The daring operation fails.

November 6 Authorities in Chicago stop a "Copperhead" (pro-Confederate) plot to disrupt the upcoming election and to burn the city.

November 8 Lincoln wins 55 percent of the popular vote and an overwhelming majority of the electoral vote when the ballots are counted on election day.

November 14 Confederate agents set fire to several New York City hotels, but little damage is done. The plot's leader, Robert Kennedy, is executed in March 1865.

November 29 Several hundred peaceful Cheyenne Indians are massacred by a Colorado militia led by Colonel John Chivington at Sand Creek, Colorado.

December 6 Following the death of Roger B. Taney, former treasury secretary Salmon Chase is appointed chief justice of the United States.

Cartoon portraying the Copperheads as a snake hissing at the fair maiden Union

December 30 Maryland politician Francis Blair urges Jefferson Davis to begin peace talks with the Union government. Davis, who had rejected all such previous proposals, later agrees to Confederate participation in a conference for peace.

• General Philip Sheridan wins a major victory at Winchester, in the Shenandoah Valley. Sheridan now begins to destroy the valley's farms to deny crops and cattle to the Confederacy.

October 19 The Confederates launch a surprise attack on Sheridan's army near Cedar Creek, Virginia. The Union troops fall back until Sheridan, away at a conference, arrives and rallies his men into a successful counterattack.

November 16 Sherman's army leaves Atlanta on its "march to the sea." Sherman intends to destroy the South's capacity to wage war; he orders his troops to kill livestock, burn crops, and tear up railroads as they advance to the coast.

December 10 Sherman's army finally reaches the Atlantic Coast just south of Savannah, Georgia; it is one the Confederacy's few remaining ports.

December 16 Months of fighting in Tennessee climax in a major Confederate defeat around Nashville and Franklin.

December 21 Sherman captures Savannah and announces his victory as a "Christmas gift" for President Lincoln.

Sherman's army destroying the railroad

A TIMELINE OF MAJOR EVENTS
January 1865–May 1865

AT HOME AND ABROAD

January 1865 Lincoln authorizes two peace missions—one by James Singleton and a second by Francis Blair—to the Confederate government. Blair proposes that the Union and Confederate armies unite to throw the French out of Mexico.

January 1 A Richmond newspaper suggests that the South put itself under the power of a European nation rather than face defeat by the Union, indicating the growing pessimism within the Confederacy.

January 11 Missouri's state government orders all slaves freed.

February 3 President Lincoln and Secretary of State William Seward meet with Confederate vice president Alexander Stephens aboard a ship off Hampton Roads, Virginia. The talks fail to make any progress toward a negotiated peace.

February 6 Former U.S. vice president John Breckinridge becomes the Confederacy's secretary of war.

February 13 British foreign minister Lord Russell protests Union military activity on the Great Lakes; Lincoln replies that the buildup is necessary to prevent raids by Confederate groups in Canada.

March 3 The U.S. Congress authorizes the Freedmen's Bureau. The agency's purpose is to help former slaves make the transition to freedom.

March 4 Lincoln is inaugurated for his second term as president. In a moving inaugural address, he announces a moderate peace policy toward the soon-to-

MILITARY EVENTS

January 16, 1865 Fort Fisher, which guards the entrance to Wilmington, North Carolina, the South's last open port, falls to Union forces.

January 31 Robert E. Lee is named commander of all Confederate forces.

February 17 Sherman's forces occupy Columbia, South Carolina; fire destroys most of the city.

February 18 Confederate forces evacuate Charleston, South Carolina. The U.S. flag is finally raised again over Fort Sumter.

March 2 Confederate general Jubal Early surrenders to Union general Philip Sheridan near Staunton, Virginia.

March 13 The Confederate Congress authorizes recruitment of black troops; few

A skirmish at Petersburg

take part in any actions.

March 28 Union forces under Grant begin their final drive on Richmond. •Union attempts to force Lee's army from the trenches around Petersburg fail at first, but Grant keeps the pressure up.

April 1 Confederate general George Pickett is defeated at Five Forks, in the opening battle be defeated Confederacy.

April 2 As Union troops approach Richmond, President Davis and his cabinet move the Confederate government to Danville, Virginia.

April 3 Escorted by black troops, President Lincoln tours Richmond shortly after its capture by Union forces.

April 7 The Union government begins talks with Great Britain in an effort to win compensation for losses to Northern shipping caused by British-built Confederate warships such as the *Alabama.*

April 10–11 Wild celebrations sweep the North following Lee's surrender. Speaking to a crowd at the White House, Lincoln reaffirms his support for a mild Reconstruction policy.

April 14 Lincoln is shot by John Wilkes Booth while attending a play at Ford's Theatre in Washington. He dies early the next morning. Secretary of State William Seward is seriously injured in another plot aimed at toppling the Union government.

April 16 Andrew Johnson is sworn in as the United States' seventeenth president.

April 17–19 Lincoln's body lies in state at the White House. April 19 is declared a national day of mourning to mark the President's death.

April 26 John Wilkes Booth, Lincoln's assassin, is trapped in a barn in the Virginia countryside. He is shot by Union soldiers and dies the next day.

John Wilkes Booth

---

of the Appomattox Campaign.

April 3 Union troops enter Richmond just after 8 a.m. By the end of the day, both Richmond and Petersburg are securely in the Union's hands.

April 4–8 Lee leads his remaining men southeast; his goal is to link up with troops under General Joseph E. Johnston. Union troops surround Lee near Appomattox Court House, Virginia.

April 9 Lee leads an unsuccessful attack on the Union forces around Appomattox. That afternoon, Lee meets with Grant and accepts his terms for the surrender of the Army of Northern Virginia.

April 9–May 25 Scattered fighting continues, especially west of the Mississippi River, but organized Confederate resistance collapses.

April 26 Confederate general Joseph E. Johnston surrenders his 30,000 troops—the last intact Southern army—to Sherman.

May 12–13 A skirmish at Palmitto Ranch, on the Rio Grande River in Texas, is the last battle of the Civil War. Ironically, it is a Confederate victory.

Appomattox Court House

Part I
Total War

Because of portraits like this one, Ulysses S. Grant was well known in the North by the end of 1864. But when Grant and his thirteen-year-old son, Fred, arrived in Washington on March 8, 1864, no one recognized the new Union commander—until he signed the register at Willard's Hotel as "U. S. Grant and son—Galena, Illinois." He quickly got the best suite in the house.

In April 1861, the Civil War began with cheering crowds, waving flags, and patriotic songs. Both sides expected a short, glorious war. By the beginning of 1864, after thirty-two months of struggle and hundreds of thousands of casualties, the glory was gone but the war remained. The Civil War had become a struggle not just between armies but between entire populations.

Victories at Vicksburg, Gettysburg, and Chattanooga had given the North the upper hand early in 1864. On battlefield after battlefield, however, the South had proved that its superior leadership and the raw courage of its soldiers could overcome greater Northern strength in men and munitions.

But the superiority of the Southern troops soon ended. The Union had a new supreme commander, Ulysses S. Grant. Under Grant, the Northern military effort gained two things it had lacked—a coordinated strategy between its eastern and western armies, and a willingness to fight Robert E. Lee's Army of Northern Virginia to the death.

In the spring of 1864, Grant confronted Lee in a series of bloody running battles outside of Richmond. Neither side had seen fighting like this before: The Army of the Potomac's losses for the week of May 5 were more than the *combined* losses Union forces had suffered in any earlier week of the war. By summer, Grant was stalled at Petersburg, Virginia. Undaunted, he settled down for a siege, while unleashing a campaign of devastation against Confederate resources in Virginia's Shenandoah Valley—a strategy that William Tecumseh Sherman repeated in Georgia.

GRANT TAKES COMMAND

In early 1864, Congress reestablished the rank of lieutenant general—last held by George Washington—and bestowed it upon Ulysses S. Grant, along with the command of the entire Union Army. On March 3, Grant left Nashville, Tennessee, to take up his new post in Washington, D.C., leaving General William Tecumseh Sherman in command of the Union forces in the West.

Grant's plan, which he hoped would finally defeat the Confederacy, was based on two strategies. The first was better coordination between Union forces in the East and West. For three years these forces had acted, Grant said, "like a balky team [of horses], no two ever pulling together." Now these two armies would act like the two fists of a boxer, coming together to smash the South, both in Georgia—the gateway to the Confederate heartland—and in Virginia. The second strategy was the destruction of Robert E. Lee's Army of Northern Virginia. Grant's orders to General George Meade, commander of the Army of the Potomac, were simple: "Wherever Lee goes, there will you go also."

But Lee, camped south of the Rapidan River with the 61,000 men of the Army of Northern Virginia, remained determined to deny Grant his ultimate goal: Richmond.

This elaborate wood-engraving (opposite, top) shows Grant (center) and the highest-ranking generals of the Army of the Potomac. Grant kept George Gordon Meade (first row; second from right) in command of the force, but announced that he himself would accompany the army in the field and direct its operations. Grant also reorganized the army and brought General Philip Sheridan from the West to command its cavalry.

Thanks to the telegraph, Grant kept in close contact with Sherman and other Western commanders during the fighting in Virginia in the spring and summer of 1864. This sketch (right) by A. R. Waud shows Grant writing out a telegraph dispatch in the field. The officer to Grant's right is probably John A. Rawlins, Grant's friend and trusted aide for most of the war.

THE RED RIVER CAMPAIGN

Even before he became overall Union commander in the spring of 1864, Grant wanted to launch an overland attack on the Confederate port of Mobile, Alabama.

President Lincoln, however, was against Grant's plan. Instead of sending Union forces around the Gulf of Mexico east to Mobile, he favored a westward advance along the Red River to Shreveport, Louisiana, and into eastern Texas. The operation would cut a cotton-rich area off from the Confederacy, but Lincoln had another motive as well. While the Union and the Confederacy were busy fighting each other, French emperor Napoleon III had landed troops in Mexico—a clear violation of the Monroe Doctrine. Lincoln hoped that the presence of the Union Army so close to Texas would give Napoleon second thoughts about turning Mexico into a French colony.

The Red River Expedition—40,000 men and fifty vessels commanded by Union general Nathaniel Banks—set out in March 1864. At first the campaign went well. Then, on April 8, a Confederate force led by General Richard Taylor defeated Banks's forces in a battle at Sabine Crossroads, Louisiana, just thirty-five miles from Shreveport. Banks decided that he had had enough and withdrew, returning to his southern Louisiana base on May 26.

The Red River Campaign failed in every respect. A French-installed ruler governed Mexico until a revolution overthrew him in 1867. More importantly, Banks's failure delayed Grant's timetable for the capture of Mobile.

Like Benjamin Butler, Nathaniel Prentiss Banks (1816–94; above) was a "political general" from Massachusetts. As a boy, he worked in a textile factory. Elected to the state legislature in 1848, he went to Congress in 1852 and became governor in 1858. He was a wealthy railroad executive as well. Unfortunately, his ability as a commander did not match his talents at business and politics.

The first battle of the Red River Campaign— an attack on Fort de Russy near Simsport, Louisiana—was a Union victory. This diagram of the fort (opposite, top) appeared in Harper's Weekly, a major Northern newspaper. It shows the fort as completed, but the structure was actually only half built when Banks's troops captured it on March 14.

This Harper's wood-engraving (right) shows the Union fleet on the Red River. The fifty vessels were nearly trapped in Confederate territory when the water level of the river began to sink. An ingenious Wisconsin colonel prevented the fleet from getting stuck on the muddy river bottom by designing temporary dams that allowed the gunboats and transports to float to safety.

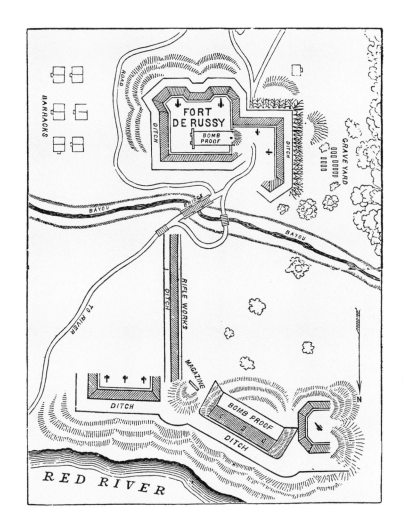

THE FORT PILLOW MASSACRE

As the war entered its third year with no end in sight, a feeling of bitterness began to creep into both armies. The South was especially angry at the use of black troops in the North. The enlistment of "slaves," announced one Confederate official, was "a barbarity." The Confederate government refused to treat captured black soldiers as prisoners of war. Instead, they were returned to their former masters or, if they had been free in the North, sold into slavery. The Union government retaliated by discontinuing prisoner exchanges with the Confederacy.

There were also several incidents in which Confederate soldiers killed captured black troops. The worst case occurred at Fort Pillow, Tennessee. Confederate cavalry leader Nathan Bedford Forrest attacked the fort on April 12, 1864. After a brief fight, the Union commander surrendered his 577-man garrison, about half of them black soldiers. The details of what followed aren't clear, but only fifty-eight blacks survived to be taken into captivity. Forrest claimed that the Union troops had tried to fight their way out of the fort and were killed in combat. Northern survivors insisted that Forrest's cavalrymen had killed scores of unarmed blacks who had surrendered.

News of the "Fort Pillow Massacre" enraged the North. Southern authorities supported Forrest's version of the event, and controversy over what actually happened continued into the twentieth century. Most historians, however, now believe that a massacre took place.

As the South's best cavalry raider, Nathan Bedford Forrest (1821–77; above) pioneered tactics that are still used by modern armies. Forrest also had great contempt for blacks. A wealthy slave trader before the war, he later helped organize the Ku Klux Klan and served as its "Grand Dragon" from 1867 to 1869.

This Northern wood-engraving (below) shows Forrest's cavalrymen killing unarmed black soldiers—and their white officers—with bayonets, sabers, and rifle butts. A letter written by Forrest stated that "The [Mississippi] river was dyed with the blood of the slaughtered for 200 yards . . . It is hoped that these facts will demonstrate to the Northern people that Negro soldiers cannot cope with Southerners."

THE BATTLE OF THE WILDERNESS

On May 4, 1864, Grant and the 122,000 men of the Army of the Potomac began crossing the Rapidan River in pursuit of Lee. By nightfall, Union troops reached the dense, gloomy forest called the Wilderness, site of their defeat a year before in the Battle of Chancellorsville.

While the Union soldiers made camp, Lee planned an attack with all the men he could find. He knew that a Confederate defeat would leave the road to Richmond open to an attack by Grant. "If victorious," Lee wrote, "we have everything to live for. If defeated, there will be nothing left to live for."

The Union Army was on the road before dawn on May 5. Shortly after, the Confederates of Richard Ewell's II Corps hit the moving Northerners, beginning the Battle of the Wilderness. Quick and determined Union resistance ruined Lee's plan for coordinated attacks on Grant's troops. The battle turned into a brutal struggle as men fought in woods so dense that they could see only a few feet ahead of them. Throughout the day, Grant sat on a log, smoking a cigar and whittling a stick, calmly issuing orders. The fighting ended at darkness with both sides still in position and the outcome still in doubt.

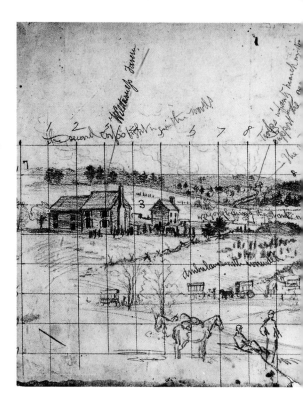

Edwin S. Forbes, a staff artist for Frank Leslie's Illustrated Newspaper, *drew this pencil sketch (above) of the Wilderness, showing the position of Union forces during the fierce two-day battle. Forbes traveled with the Army of the Potomac from the spring of 1861 to the summer of 1864, depicting each of its major battles for Northern readers. Forbes said that his role in combat was "nearly as dangerous as being a participant."*

This Kurz & Allison lithograph shows Union and Confederate cavalry clashing as the Battle of the Wilderness begins (right). If Lee had been able to concentrate his scattered forces and strike along the right side of the Army of the Potomac as he had planned, he might have won a Southern victory. Grant and Meade, however, refused to give Lee time or space to maneuver, and the jungle-like terrain of the Wilderness made movement of any kind difficult and dangerous.

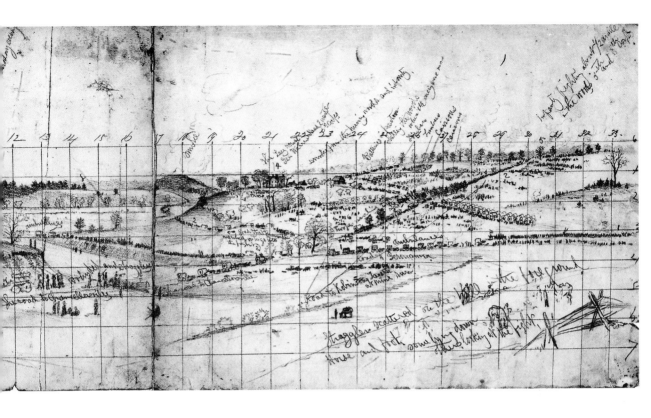

OUT OF THE WILDERNESS

On the morning of May 6, a force of 20,000 Union soldiers led by Winfield Scott Hancock attacked two Confederate divisions. By 7:00 a.m., Hancock's men had broken through the Confederate line. "We are driving them, Sir!" Hancock told Meade.

But the Confederates regrouped and, aided by a newly arrived Texas brigade, counterattacked. By the afternoon, Hancock's men were almost back where they had started. Confederate general James Longstreet then sent four brigades along an unfinished railroad bed—a path the Union commanders didn't know about—and struck Hancock's exhausted troops in a surprise attack. The Northerners were almost defeated, but the dense woods broke the force of the Southern assault. The Confederates faltered when Longstreet fell wounded with a bullet in his shoulder.

By nightfall the battle was over. The Army of the Potomac hadn't been defeated—but with 18,000 Union casualties, the Battle of the Wilderness could hardly be called a victory. Would the Union Army withdraw north to safety, as it had done so many times before?

On the evening of May 7, the Army of the Potomac began a nighttime march. The leading troops reached a crossroads where northbound and southbound roads met. Their officers led them onto the southbound road, away from Union territory, and a cheer went up: The Army of the Potomac was going to continue the fight.

Sparks from rifles and cannons set the dry underbrush of the Wilderness on fire in many places, threatening wounded men with an agonizing death. As shown in this A. R. Waud sketch (above), troops raced to rescue wounded from the burning woods. "Some were carried off by the ambulance corps, others in blankets suspended from four muskets, and more by aid of sticks, muskets, and even crawling," wrote a Northern reporter.

The last Confederate attack in the Wilderness, shown in this sketch (right), came late on the afternoon of May 6, when John B. Gordon led his brigade of Georgians against the Union left flank. Gordon's men advanced as far as Brock Road. When Meade heard that the Confederates had broken the Union line, he snorted, "If they have broken our lines, they can do no more tonight." As Meade expected, Gordon's attack stalled as night fell.

between 4 and 5 P M - 9th May - 64

Rebel advance through the smoke and seizing a part of the breast work on Brock road - The logs had caught fire - ARW.

SPOTSYLVANIA

Lee realized that Grant's next goal would be Spotsylvania Court House, twelve miles southeast of the Wilderness in Virginia. The roads on which Lee depended for supplies ran through the town. If Grant captured it, Lee's already hungry army would be cut off from food and ammunition.

Both armies raced for the important junction. Confederate cavalry under Fitzhugh Lee, Robert E. Lee's nephew, reached it first, and held it until the Southern infantry arrived. Lee's soldiers quickly dug an elaborate network of trenches and earthworks. On May 8 and 9, Grant and Meade ordered attacks in an effort to go through, or around, Lee's defenses.

On May 10, a young Union colonel, Emery Upton, led twelve regiments against a section of the Confederate defenses called the Mule Shoe. Using new tactics of his own invention, Upton broke through the Southern line and took about a thousand prisoners. The troops assigned to follow up this breakthrough, however, failed to move forward, and the Confederates recaptured the Mule Shoe at the end of the day.

Despite the setback, Upton's brief success encouraged Grant. He decided to apply the same tactics in an assault by an entire corps. That night, he wrote to Union chief of staff Henry Halleck, "I propose to fight it out on this line if it takes all summer."

Despite their ordeal at the Wilderness, the Army of the Potomac cheered Grant (above) when they learned that their new leader intended to give Lee a fight to the finish. "If you see the President," Grant told a Northern reporter returning to Washington from the Wilderness, "tell him, from me, that whatever happens, there will be no turning back."

Furious hand-to-hand combat marked the fighting at Spotsylvania, as shown in this lithograph published by Prang & Co. (opposite, top). Among the casualties of the first two days was John Sedgwick, one of the Union's best generals. Attempting to rally his men, Sedgwick stood up and said, "They couldn't hit an elephant at this distance!" Within a minute, he was killed by a bullet from a Confederate sharpshooter.

This map (right) shows the positions of Union and Confederate forces around the Spotsylvania Courthouse. While the infantry on both sides were locked in brutal combat, cavalry clashed along nearby roads. On May 11, Union cavalrymen led by General Philip Sheridan attacked Lee's cavalry at Yellow Tavern, near Richmond. Among the dead in the battle that followed was J.E.B. Stuart, leader of the Army of Northern Virginia's horsemen.

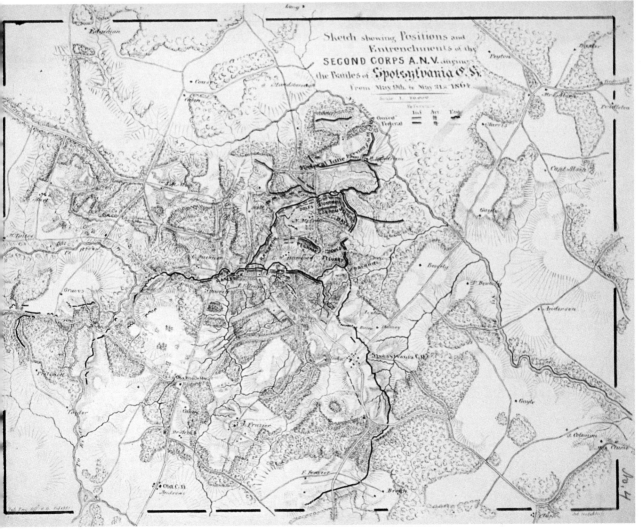

Sketch showing Positions and Entrenchments of the SECOND CORPS A.N.V. during the Battles of Spotsylvania C.H. from May 9th to May 21st 1864.

SPOTSYLVANIA: THE OUTCOME

On May 11, Lee's scouts reported that Union wagons were on the move. Believing that Grant was attempting to outflank him, Lee ordered most of his artillery out of the Confederate front line. When night fell and the Union troops remained in position, Lee realized that his guess was wrong. He quickly brought the artillery back up—but it was too late. Shortly before daybreak, the 20,000 troops of Winfield Scott Hancock's corps assaulted the Confederate line, broke it, and split Lee's army in half. The road to Richmond appeared open at last.

The Army of Northern Virginia, however, was not ready to give up. Lee sent every available man into the fray, including a division kept in reserve for just such an emergency. Lee himself rode forward to lead the defense, but his devoted men, refusing to let him expose himself to danger, grabbed the bridle of his horse and turned it back around.

By noon, Hancock's men were back at their starting point, but Grant and Meade renewed the attack on Lee's left and right flanks. Eventually, the Union and Confederate lines met at an angle, and savage hand-to-hand fighting continued until midnight.

Grant ordered a new assault on the morning of May 13, but when the Union troops went forward they found the Confederate trenches abandoned. Lee had withdrawn.

In this Currier & Ives lithograph (above), Hancock's corps begin an early-morning assault—just in time to capture the twenty cannons Lee had ordered back into position. The eighteen hours of combat that followed were among the most cruel and costly of the entire war. The fighting on May 12 alone left 6,800 Union soldiers dead or wounded; there were nearly 5,000 Confederate casualties. One of the Union survivors wrote in his diary, "This has been the most terrible day I have ever lived."

This photograph (right) by Timothy O'Sullivan shows Grant (seated with legs crossed, between the two trees) and Meade (studying a map) meeting with their staffs outside Massaponax, Virginia, on May 21, as the Army of the Potomac moved south away from Spotsylvania. The officers are seated on pews dragged out of nearby Massaponax Church.

THE ARMIES APPROACH COLD HARBOR

After a week of fighting at Spotsylvania, both armies turned south. Union and Confederate forces now clashed every day as Grant advanced deeper into Virginia, and Lee tried desperately to stop him. The exhausted soldiers of the Army of the Potomac, in uniforms caked with mud, sweat, and blood, moved south in a series of marches around the flanks of Lee's moving army.

As May ended, Grant approached Cold Harbor. Although Cold Harbor was just a run-down crossroads tavern, Lee and Grant both realized its importance. It was only eight miles from Richmond; if Grant maneuvered Lee into a decisive fight so close to the Confederate capital, he could destroy the Army of Northern Virginia and link up with Union reinforcements moving inland from the Pamunkey River.

Once again, the two armies raced toward a single objective, and once again the Confederate cavalry reached it first. Union horsemen drove them out, but Confederate infantry recaptured the vital crossroads. On June 1, a Union assault against Cold Harbor failed, with heavy casualties. Grant ordered another attack for the next day.

By the time the Battle of Cold Harbor began, the soldiers of both armies were suffering from the exhaustion and shock of a month of almost continuous battle. Lee's forces now numbered about 60,000 men; Union strength stood at 109,000. "Many a man," wrote a young Union officer, "has gone crazy since this campaign began from the terrible pressure on mind & body." In this lithograph, men of the Army of the Potomac's VI and XVIII corps attack the Confederate positions at Cold Harbor.

THE BATTLE OF COLD HARBOR

The attack, planned for June 2, did not take place. The leading unit, the Union's II Corps, was exhausted from its all-night march to the battlefield and failed to get into position on schedule. Grant decided to make an even larger assault on June 3.

The Confederates used the twenty-four-hour delay wisely. They dug trenches and built earthworks to blunt the Union attack. The men of the Army of the Potomac knew what they would be up against. On the night of June 2, a Union officer watched soldiers, "calmly writing their names . . . on slips of paper and pinning them to their coats, so that their bodies might be recognized and their fate made known to their families at home."

At 4:30 a.m. on June 3, 50,000 Union soldiers moved forward along a two-mile front. Lee had rushed in reinforcements from all over Virginia, and Confederate resistance was far heavier than expected. "The dreadful storm of lead and iron seemed more like a volcanic blast than a battle," wrote a Northern soldier. In less than thirty minutes, 7,000 Union troops lay dead or wounded in front of the Confederate earthworks.

The assault was a total failure—and yet Grant ordered another attack two hours later. The men ordered into action refused to move. Grant realized his mistake and told his staff, "I regret this assault more than any I have ever ordered."

Northern units captured parts of the Confederate line on the morning of June 3, but their success proved temporary because of the confusion of battle and the vagueness of Grant's orders. This A. R. Waud sketch (right) shows the 7th New York Heavy Artillery seizing Lee's forward trenches. (The Army of the Potomac's "heavy artillery" regiments were supposed to guard the forts protecting Washington, but Grant ordered them into Virginia to fight as infantry.)

Winfield Scott Hancock (1824–86; below), seated here with his staff at Cold Harbor, was one of the Army of the Potomac's ablest commanders. He fought bravely at Chancellorsville in May 1863, and his actions at Gettysburg in July of that year helped turn a potential Union defeat into victory. Throughout the fighting in Virginia in 1864, Hancock was in pain from an unhealed wound suffered at Gettysburg.

7th N.Y. Heavy Arty. in Barlow's charge in Cold Harbor Friday June 3rd 1864.

CONFEDERATE COMMERCE RAIDERS

Although the Confederacy didn't have an official deep water navy, it did have a fleet of "commerce raiders," heavily-armed ships that roamed the oceans of the world sinking or capturing any ship flying the Union flag. Many of these raiders were built for the Confederate government by British shipyards, a major sore point between the Union and British governments. In September 1863, after a long diplomatic campaign by U.S. minister Charles Francis Adams, the British government finally agreed to stop the practice.

By that time, however, nineteen Confederate commerce raiders were operating. Together they had destroyed or captured almost 200 Northern merchant ships carrying cargoes valued at more than $13 million. These losses caused insurance brokers to raise rates by several hundred percent, forcing many Northern shipping companies out of business. Others registered their ships with neutral countries so that they could sail safely. It took the American merchant fleet, which in 1861 was beginning to overtake Britain's fleet in size and importance, over fifty years to recover from the effects of the war.

The most famous and successful Confederate raider was the *Alabama*, commanded by Captain Raphael Semmes. Sixty Northern ships had fallen victim to Semmes before the Union warship *Kearsarge* engaged the *Alabama* in battle in the English Channel on June 19, 1864.

During the Mexican War, Maryland-born Raphael Semmes (1809–77; left) shared a cabin with fellow U.S. Navy officer John Winslow (1811–73). Semmes resigned from active service after Fort Sumter to sail for the Confederacy. Winslow remained in the Union Navy and eventually faced his former cabinmate in battle as commander of the Kearsarge.

The Alabama was built in Liverpool, England, and launched on May 15, 1862. Charles Francis Adams persuaded the British government to forbid the Alabama from leaving port, but by the time the order reached Liverpool the ship was already at sea. The Alabama's two-year voyage took Captain Semmes and his mostly English crew from Singapore to the West Indies and finally to the coast of France, where the Kearsarge sank her, as shown in this painting (below).

THE *ALABAMA* AND THE *KEARSARGE*

The *Alabama* arrived in Cherbourg, France, in June 1864 to drop off prisoners from captured Yankee vessels and take on supplies. A few days later, the Union warship *Kearsarge*, commanded by Captain John Winslow, arrived and waited for the *Alabama* to depart.

On the morning of June 19, the *Alabama* steamed into the English Channel. Crowds of people watched from ashore. The fight began when Semmes sent a flurry of shots crashing into the *Kearsarge*.

The battle lasted just over an hour. Semmes, finally realizing that his own guns were doing little harm to the Union warship, ordered the badly damaged *Alabama* back into port. When it was clear that the rapidly sinking ship would never make it to safety, Semmes had the Confederate flag hauled down and the crew abandoned ship. An English yacht took Semmes and other survivors to England, where a Southern officer wrote, "we were received with every kindness and sympathy." Of the *Alabama*'s 149 sailors, three were killed and nine wounded; on the *Kearsarge*, only three men were wounded.

So ended the career of the South's most notorious raider. Others continued to harass Union ships until after the end of the war. The *Shenandoah*, unaware of the Confederate surrender in April 1865, destroyed eight Northern ships before surrendering in Liverpool in November.

This illustration shows Union gunners aboard the Kearsarge watching as the Alabama begins to sink. The two ships were not especially well matched. In the words of John Kell, the Alabama's executive officer, "The Kearsarge was . . . a man of war, staunch and well-built; the Alabama was made for flight and speed and was much more lightly constructed than her chosen antagonist." The Kearsarge was also armored, something Semmes was not aware of when he decided to fight the Union vessel.

THE PETERSBURG CAMPAIGN BEGINS

In early June, the Army of Northern Virginia, battered after the month of battles at the Wilderness, Spotsylvania, and Cold Harbor, still defiantly blocked the way into Richmond. Grant now realized that head-on attacks like the one at Cold Harbor would only continue to weaken his army—and the spirit of the Northern public.

Grant decided that the key to Richmond was Petersburg, a city of 18,000 people twenty-three miles southeast of the Confederate capital. The city was the hub of the network of roads and railroads that supplied Richmond—and Lee's army. Grant hoped that taking Petersburg would shatter the Confederacy's ability to wage war in Virginia. On June 11, Grant began moving the army south from Cold Harbor. The soldiers crossed the broad James River on a 2,100-foot-long pontoon bridge four days later.

A complex network of trenches and fortifications protected Petersburg, but only a handful of Confederates, under P.G.T. Beauregard, held them. Lee, believing that Richmond was still Grant's true goal, at first refused Beauregard's pleas for reinforcements. A well-coordinated Northern assault could easily have taken the city. Unfortunately, the first attacks on Petersburg were clumsy and timid. Lee, now awake to the danger, moved the Army of Northern Virginia into the city on June 18. Once again, Lee had beaten Grant in a race for a vital stronghold.

Grant's original plan to capture Petersburg called for General Benjamin Butler's 33,000-man army to move up the James River and cut the rail lines around the city. However Butler (left) allowed himself to be cornered by the outnumbered Confederates on a peninsula called Bermuda Hundred. Butler's army was trapped, "as if it had been in a bottle strongly corked." Butler was one of the Union's worst generals, but because he was an influential politician, Lincoln couldn't fire him.

From June 18 to June 22, Grant and Meade launched a series of fruitless attacks against Confederate positions protecting Petersburg, shown in this sketch (below). A New York private described an attack: "The line of blue swept forward in good order, cheering loudly . . . Then the heads of Lee's infantry rose above their entrenchments. I saw the glint of the sun on their polished rifle barrels. Our men began to tumble in large numbers."

PETERSBURG: THE CRATER

In July, generals Grant and Meade declared that the campaign for Petersburg would continue by "regular approaches." The Northerners built lines of trenches, forts, and gun pits that quickly surpassed those held by Lee's men.

The Army of the Potomac made one more attempt to storm its way into Petersburg. A regiment of Pennsylvania coal miners came up with a plan to dig a tunnel packed with explosives under one of the main Confederate forts. Once the fort was blown up, Union troops would storm through the gap in Lee's lines.

The tunnel was completed on July 23. On July 30, at 4:40 a.m., 8,000 pounds of gunpowder exploded, creating a crater 200 feet long and 50 feet deep. The first part of the plan had worked. The second—the assault through the gap—failed miserably. The spearhead of the assault was supposed to be a division of specially-trained black troops. At the last minute, they were replaced by a white unit whose commander stayed behind—drunk— during the attack. The Union troops milled around in the crater instead of moving through it, and the Confederates quickly counterattacked, shooting at the trapped men from the rim of the crater. The black troops finally moved forward, only to be cut down by Southern fire. The "Battle of the Crater" ended with no other result than 3,500 Union casualties.

The miners of the 48th Pennsylvania built a tunnel under Confederate trenches that eventually measured 510 feet, making it the longest military tunnel up to that time. The miners had to pick their way forward by candlelight, as shown in this engraving (above).

It took several tries before the fuse was finally lit, but when the explosion came it was spectacular (right). A Union officer described it: "A vast cloud of earth is borne upward, one hundred feet in the air, presenting the appearance of an outspread umbrella, descending in a twinkling of an eye with a heavy thud!"

THE VALLEY CAMPAIGN BEGINS

In April 1864, Grant ordered General Franz Sigel to lead 23,000 Union troops into Virginia's Shenandoah Valley. Sigel's job was to capture Lee's supply depot at Lynchburg, and to keep the Confederates from using the valley as a highway for raids into the North. On May 14, Sigel ran into a Confederate force under Major General John C. Breckinridge, a former U.S. vice president, at New Market. After a hard-fought battle in a thunderstorm, Sigel retreated. On May 19, both the Union and Confederate armies in the valley changed commanders. Breckinridge went south to join Lee, with Jubal Early taking his place, while Grant replaced Sigel with David Hunter.

Hunter's troops moved up the valley from the south, burning farms and looting houses along the way. While Hunter's actions had a military purpose—the fertile valley fed Lee's army—they caused much suffering and bitterness. Many of the valley's people were members of pacifist religious groups. For years they had tried to stay out of the way of the fighting that raged around them. Now destruction had come to their land, and it would only get worse.

On June 18, Hunter and Early clashed near Lynchburg, Virginia. Defeated, Hunter not only retreated but withdrew his army westward into the Blue Ridge Mountains, leaving the valley wide open to the Confederates.

The high point of the Battle of New Market came when General John Breckinridge (1821–75; above) reluctantly sent a unit of 200 cadets from the Virginia Military Institute to plug a hole in the Confederate battle line. The cadets—some as young as fifteen—charged through a storm of Union fire, filled the gap, and captured a Union cannon. Ten cadets died and forty-seven fell wounded at New Market.

Like Benjamin Butler, German-born Franz Sigel (opposite, top) owed his rank more to politics than to military skill. A St. Louis school superintendent before the war, he helped keep Missouri from seceding in 1861. He was quickly promoted to general, in part to help Union recruiting efforts among German Americans. Some 175,000 German-born soldiers eventually served in the Union Army.

The 150-mile-long Shenandoah Valley was called "the Granary of the Confederacy." Its efficient farms provided food not only for the Army of Northern Virginia, but for Richmond. David Hunter and his successor, Philip Sheridan, oversaw the destruction of much of the valley to keep its resources from aiding the Confederacy. In this print (right), Union soldiers burn a flour mill.

JUBAL EARLY RAIDS WASHINGTON

Lee took advantage of Hunter's defeat by sending Early and 10,000 men up the valley toward Washington. Lee knew that Early could never capture the city, but he hoped that Grant would be forced to send troops north to deal with the threat—away from Petersburg.

Jubal Early crossed the Potomac on July 6. A small force under General Lew Wallace slowed the raiders but failed to stop them. In Maryland, they paused to burn the Silver Springs home of Union postmaster general Montgomery Blair. A few days later Early crossed into the District of Columbia.

The Union capital was almost undefended; Grant had taken every ablebodied soldier out of the city to fight in Virginia. Union officers in the capital rounded up the recuperating wounded and soldiers on leave to guard the forts protecting the city. In the meantime, Grant sent the Army of the Potomac's VI Corps back to Washington by water.

At noon on July 11, Early's troops reached Fort Stevens. They were within sight of the newly-completed capitol dome in Washington. The defenders and attackers traded shots all day as President Lincoln watched. Early withdrew only after Grant's veteran troops finally arrived to take over the fort's defense.

The raid did nothing more than scare the North, but it made Grant more determined to deny the Shenandoah Valley to the Confederates.

Jubal Early (1816–94; left) was described by one of his staff as "disagreeable . . . he made few admirers or friends either by his manners or his habits." As a young officer, Early was jilted by his fiancée, leaving him with a low opinion of women. Hearing that the wife of a fellow Confederate general had narrowly escaped capture by a Union patrol, he said he was sorry she had been allowed to get away.

Abraham Lincoln watches Early's attack on Fort Stevens in this engraving (below)—although he was actually inside the fort and not on horseback during the battle. The president stood up several times to get a better look at the fighting. Union captain Oliver Wendell Holmes, Jr., a future Supreme Court chief justice, got angry. Not realizing who the tall civilian was, Holmes shouted, "Get down, you damn fool, before you get shot!" Lincoln smiled and sat down.

THE VALLEY CAMPAIGN: WINCHESTER

On August 1, Grant issued orders to General Philip Sheridan, commander of the Army of the Potomac's cavalry. Sheridan was "to put himself south of [Jubal Early] and follow him to the death." Besides clearing Confederates out of the valley, Sheridan was to destroy the cattle and crops that fed Lee's army. Sheridan's men, wrote Grant, should "eat out Virginia clear and clean as far as they go, so that crows flying over it . . . will have to carry their [food] with them."

Sheridan moved cautiously at first. Then word came from Quaker schoolteacher Rebecca Wright that part of Early's force had left the valley to join Lee. The remaining 15,000 Confederates were camped along Opequon Creek near the town of Winchester. Sheridan attacked with his 37,000 soldiers on September 19. After a furious eight-hour battle, Early retreated north up the valley to Fisher's Hill. Sheridan drove them off the hill on September 22. Again Early retreated, this time deep into the Blue Ridge Mountains.

Sheridan now turned his attention to his second task—destroying the region's resources. On October 7, Sheridan reported that the Union Army of the Shenandoah had "destroyed over 2,000 barns filled with wheat, hay, and farming implements . . . over seventy mills filled with flour and wheat; have driven in front of the army over 3,000 head of stock . . . "

A reporter described five-foot-six Philip Sheridan (1831–88; left) as a "little mountain of combative force." It was not Sheridan's height, but his age—thirty-three—that led Lincoln to question Grant's judgment in giving him the job of clearing the Shenandoah Valley. Grant, however, insisted that the valley command go to his most aggressive cavalry chief.

The Battle of Opequon Creek ended in a wild cavalry charge and, as shown in this painting (below), Sheridan was in the forefront. Early's men finally broke and fled through Winchester, Virginia, leaving 2,000 dead and wounded and 2,000 prisoners to the Union. "We have just sent them whirling through Winchester," Sheridan telegraphed Grant that night, "and we are after them tomorrow."

THE VALLEY CAMPAIGN: CEDAR CREEK

Jubal Early refused to admit defeat. Taking advantage of a break in the fighting around Petersburg, Lee sent reinforcements to the valley, bringing Early's strength up to 21,000 men. Just before dawn on October 19, Early and his men caught the Union troops by surprise at their camp along Cedar Creek in Virginia. By mid-morning Sheridan's army was in full retreat.

Sheridan, however, wasn't with them. He was on the road from Winchester, after attending a conference in Washington, when he heard the news of Early's attack. Spurring his black horse, Rienzi, into a gallop, he rode toward the sound of the guns.

He soon encountered signs of defeat—wounded, dispirited soldiers staggering away from battle. A few men cheered as he approached. "Damn you, don't you cheer me!" Sheridan cried out. "If you love your country, come up to the front!" Then he reached the main body of his fleeing army. By the sheer force of his personality, Sheridan turned the men around to face Early's Confederates.

Back at Cedar Creek, Early's famished troops had halted their attack to eat the rations of the retreating Northerners. At 4:00 p.m., the sound of thundering hooves and cheering men split the air. It was Sheridan and his men, attacking along a two-mile front. By sundown, the Union troops were back in the camp they had fled at dawn. Early and his surviving troops retreated down the valley to New Market. The valley was finally clear.

Sheridan's officers, including George Custer, display Confederate battle flags captured during the Valley Campaign in this sketch (right). Custer (second from left) graduated from West Point—last in his class—just in time to join the Union Army. By the end of the war he was a brevet major general. (Brevets were battlefield promotions, usually temporary.) Custer stayed in the army after the war, finally meeting his end at the Battle of the Little Bighorn in 1876.

Sheridan's twenty-mile ride from Winchester to Cedar Creek was the inspiration for a popular poem by Thomas B. Read. It was also the subject of countless wood-engravings, lithographs, and paintings. This painting (below) shows Sheridan rallying his men just before the counterattack at Cedar Creek. When Sheridan rode into sight, a Union private later wrote, "No more doubt or chance for doubt existed. We were safe . . . and every man knew it."

Part II
Nearing the End

David Glasgow Farragut (1801–70) gave the U.S. Navy one of its most enduring catchphrases—"Damn the torpedoes, full speed ahead"—during the Battle of Mobile Bay on August 5, 1864. In 1861, the Tennessee-born Farragut had to overcome suspicion regarding his Southern origins in order to win high command in the Union Navy. He proved to be the North's greatest naval commander.

By the fall of 1864, the number of Confederate troops was dwindling from desertion and casualties, and Southern civilians were feeling the effects of the increasingly successful Union blockade. But war weariness was growing in the North, too. Grant's spring offensive in Virginia had led only to drawn-out trench warfare at Petersburg. In the West, Sherman's army held Atlanta under siege but still failed to take the city, even after months of campaigning.

Many people in the North, including the president himself, believed that the Republicans faced defeat in the upcoming presidential election. Because the Democratic Party favored a negotiated peace with the Confederacy, the hope of a Democratic victory fueled Confederate resistance at Atlanta and Petersburg. Then, on September 2, Sherman captured Atlanta, helping to ensure presidential victory for Lincoln. The war could now end only if the Confederacy was defeated.

Sherman further crippled the South's faltering economy with his devastating marches through Georgia and the Carolinas. When the spring of 1865 came, Lee launched one final, unsuccessful offensive at Petersburg. Then, on April 3, Richmond fell. Jefferson Davis escaped the capital and urged further resistance, but on April 9 Lee surrendered to Grant at Appomattox Court House. General Joseph E. Johnston surrendered his army in the Carolinas to Sherman seventeen days later.

Except for minor fighting in the West, the war was over. Peace would bring new challenges, but the man best qualified to lead the reunited nation forward—Abraham Lincoln—lay dead from an assassin's bullet five days after Lee's surrender at Appomattox.

THE BATTLE OF MOBILE BAY

With Nathaniel Banks's troops skirmishing with the Confederates along the Red River, the task of overtaking Mobile went to the Union Navy. The city of Mobile itself, which lay thirty miles north of the entrance to Mobile Bay, was not the target. Control of the bay would be enough to shut down the port—the Confederacy's last remaining harbor on the Gulf of Mexico.

Command of the Mobile Expedition went to sixty-three-year-old Admiral David Glasgow Farragut, the officer who had captured New Orleans in 1862. Farragut assembled an intimidating fleet—fourteen large wooden warships and four smaller ironclad gunboats.

The bay's defenses consisted of three forts—Morgan, Gaines, and Powell—overlooking the narrow three-mile entrance to the bay. A Confederate fleet waited within Mobile Bay. Most of the southern vessels were hastily improvised gunboats, but among them was the powerful ironclad *Tennessee*.

At 5:45 a.m. on August 5, the Union fleet steamed forward toward the bay's narrow entrance. Signal Lieutenant John Kinney, aboard the *Hartford*, described the opening of the battle: "A light breeze had scattered the fog and left a clear, sunny August day. The line moved slowly, and it was an hour before starting that the opening gun was fired. This was a fifteen-inch shell from the [Union ironclad] *Tecumseh*, and it exploded over Fort Morgan."

Farragut's fleet steams into Mobile Bay through a storm of Confederate fire in this 1886 print. Smoke from the guns of the forts and ships soon grew so thick that Farragut had to climb into the rigging of his flagship, the Hartford, to observe the battle.

VICTORY FOR THE UNION FLEET

As Farragut's warships moved toward the bay's entrance, the ironclad *Tecumseh* hit a torpedo (mine) and sank. The entire Union fleet stopped in the water, the captains suddenly afraid to move forward. But the vessels couldn't stay where they were—the guns of Fort Morgan had begun sweeping their decks with cannonballs. "Shot after shot came through the side," wrote a Union officer on the *Hartford*, "mowing down the men, deluging the decks with blood and scattering mingled fragments of humanity so thickly that it was difficult to stand on the deck, so slippery was it."

Farragut realized that the fleet had to keep moving, even though it meant risking more losses to torpedoes. "Damn the torpedoes! Full speed ahead!" shouted the admiral. The fleet couldn't hear him over the roar of the guns, but when the *Hartford* steamed forward, the rest of the Union vessels followed.

Once inside the bay, the Union warships destroyed or drove off every ship in the Confederate fleet, including the much-feared *Tennessee*. Union losses for the battle totaled 145 killed and 170 wounded.

Over the next three weeks, the fleet—aided by 2,000 soldiers—captured the three forts surrounding the bay. By the end of August, the port of Mobile was closed for good.

When the Union ironclad Tecumseh *sank (right), it took 93 of its 114 crew members to the bottom of Mobile Bay. Like all small ironclad gunboats, the* Tecumseh *was known as a "Monitor," after the Union's first ironclad warship, launched in 1862.*

The climax of the battle in Mobile Bay came when the Confederate ironclad Tennessee *moved out to meet Farragut's fleet (shown in the wood-engraving below). Besides its heavy guns, the* Tennessee's *bow was thickly armored for use as a ram—making the Confederate vessel a double threat to the Union's wooden-hulled warships. The* Tennessee's *size made it hard to maneuver, however, and the ironclad surrendered when Union gunners shot away its rudder.*

SHERMAN TURNS TO GEORGIA

In March 1864, Grant had traveled to Cincinnati, Ohio, to plan strategy with William Tecumseh Sherman. As always, Grant's orders were simple. He told Sherman to "get into the interior of the enemy's country as far as you can, inflicting all the damage you can against their war resources."

This meant taking Atlanta, Georgia's capital and the "Gate City of the South." Aside from being the hub of a road and rail network, Atlanta was one of the Confederacy's few industrial cities. Seizing the city would open the Southern heartland to Union forces and cripple much of the Confederacy's ability to wage war.

On May 4, the beginning of a long campaign to capture Atlanta, Sherman began moving down from Tennessee with a force of 100,000 men, divided into three separate armies. Opposing him were 45,000 Confederate troops under Joseph E. Johnston. A calculating defensive fighter, Johnston held a line along the rocky terrain around Dalton, Georgia.

Johnston hoped that Sherman would attack him head-on, but the Union general had other plans. Sherman sideslipped his force toward Atlanta, forcing Johnston's Confederates out of the mountains. The two armies maneuvered around each other in what one historian called "a formalized military dance performed to the rhythmic music of the guns." Sherman tried to attack Johnston's troops at Kenesaw Mountain on June 27. The assault failed with heavy casualties, and the war of maneuvers continued.

On July 21, Confederate general Benjamin Cheatham's corps attacked a Union force led by General James McPherson, one of Sherman's best commanders. McPherson was killed in the battle, and Sherman wept openly when he heard of his death. Cheatham is shown directing his troops in this sketch (right).

In this illustration (below), Union general John Logan (on horseback) watched as his troops stormed the Southern positions on 700-foot-high Kenesaw Mountain. Sherman called off the assault after losing 3,000 men in a matter of hours. The 100-degree temperature added to the misery of both the attackers and defenders. "I never saw so many broken-down and exhausted men in my life," wrote a Confederate soldier after the battle.

ATLANTA
HOLDS OUT

Johnston's defense of Atlanta was masterful: He blocked Sherman at every turn, slowing the Union Army's progress. Nevertheless, by July 8, part of the Union Army was across the Chattahoochee River, the last major natural obstacle protecting Atlanta.

Jefferson Davis and other Confederate officials didn't fully realize the effectiveness of Johnston's strategy. Believing that the only way to save Atlanta was to destroy Sherman's army, Davis replaced Johnston with the more aggressive John Bell Hood on July 17.

Three days after taking command, Hood struck Union general George Thomas's Army of the Cumberland, part of which was about to cross Peachtree Creek just three miles from Atlanta. Hood moved fast, but not fast enough. Thomas's troops were safely across the creek when the attack came, and they drove the Southerners off. Hood attacked twice in the following week, losing 18,000 men—almost one third of his force. Finally, Hood withdrew his men into the trenches and fortifications protecting Atlanta.

Despite Hood's failures, Atlanta held out. Jefferson Davis was more determined than ever to save the city, now a symbol of hope to the embattled Confederacy. The loss of Atlanta, in his words, would "open the way for the Federal [Union] Army to the Gulf on one hand, and to Charleston on the other, and close up those rich granaries . . . It would give them control of our network of railways and thus paralyze our efforts."

No one on either side doubted the bravery of John Bell Hood (left), who was wounded many times in battle. Union general John Schofield, who had been Hood's roommate at West Point, told Sherman, "He'll hit you like hell before you know it." But some of Hood's fellow Confederates questioned his ability. Robert E. Lee described him as, "All lion, none of the fox."

The last major battle in the campaign for Atlanta was fought twenty miles south of the city, at Jonesboro, Georgia. Hood's Confederates attempted to drive the Union troops out of Jonesboro on August 31 and again on September 1, both times without success. This Currier & Ives lithograph (below) of the event appeared less than two months after the battle.

THE SIEGE OF ATLANTA

Following Hood's unsuccessful attempts to push back the Union Army, Sherman sent troops around Atlanta to cut off the four major railroads passing through the city. Three railroads fell into Union possession, but one—the Macon & Western—remained in Confederate hands, giving Atlanta a lifeline to the rest of the Confederacy. Sherman realized that Atlanta would have to be taken by siege.

The campaign for Atlanta had taken on political as well as military significance. The war was now well into its third year, and the Northern public was growing weary. Grant remained stuck in the trenches at Petersburg. It seemed that the North had nothing to show for the terrible casualties of the spring of 1864. Unless the Union won a major victory, Lincoln would almost surely be defeated in the upcoming presidential election.

Pressure was on Sherman to win such a victory at Atlanta. While his cavalry continued to clash with Hood's troops, Union infantry and artillery dug lines of trenches around Atlanta. Soon Sherman's guns were pounding the city. By mid-August, many of Atlanta's citizens were on the road as refugees, fleeing the relentless Union bombardment.

On August 25, Sherman withdrew most of his men from their trenches and sent them moving south of Atlanta. Hood sent 24,000 men under General William Hardee after them. Hardee's force was defeated at Jonesboro. Atlanta was now bound to fall.

During the siege of Atlanta, Johnston concentrated his forces south of the Etowah River, shown in the above photo, especially around rocky Altoona Pass. Sherman, however, avoided an attack on the heavily defended pass and instead moved his army though Dallas, a road junction twelve miles away.

This map (opposite, top) shows the positions of Johnston's and Sherman's forces during the siege. At some points, the Union line was barely a mile from the city. Because Confederate supply depots and other military targets were scattered throughout Atlanta, the entire city came under fire from Sherman's artillery.

On August 9, nearly 5,000 Union shells fell on Atlanta (right), causing the death of six civilians. Sherman (shown with binoculars) regretted the civilian casualties, but believed that they were unavoidable because the city refused to surrender. "War is war, and not popularity-seeking," he wrote in his memoirs.

THE FALL OF ATLANTA

With Hardee defeated and the Macon & Western Railroad finally cut, Hood faced the bitter truth: He had to abandon Atlanta to save what remained of his army. "On the night of September 1," he reported sadly to Jefferson Davis, "we withdrew from Atlanta." On that night, the men of General Henry Slocum's XX Corps, a unit of the Army of the Potomac sent to fight Sherman's Western army, heard explosions and felt the earth around their trenches shake. It was Hood's men blowing up their own ammunition.

In the morning, the men of the XX Corps marched into Atlanta with flags flying and bands playing, and soon the Union flag waved above city hall. The next day, Sherman arrived and sent a joyful telegram to Washington: "So Atlanta is ours, and fairly won."

The fall of Atlanta swept away the cloud of gloom in the North. Lincoln offered Sherman the nation's thanks. Dozens of Northern cities fired hundred-gun salutes. Grant announced that Sherman's achievement was "unsurpassed if not unequaled."

Spirits fell when word of Atlanta's capture spread through the Confederacy. "Never until now did I feel hopeless," wrote one Southerner, "but since God seems to have forsaken us, I despair."

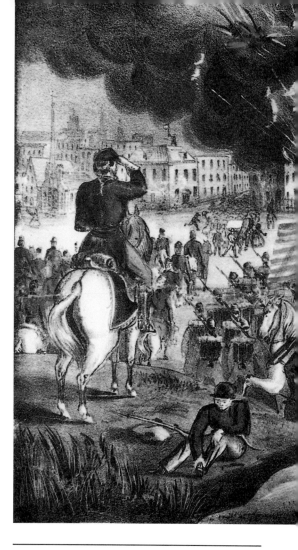

This vivid but inaccurate lithograph (above) shows the first Union troops—General Slocum's XX Corps—entering Atlanta on September 2. Most of Sherman's soldiers were from Western states such as Indiana and Illinois, and at first they had ridiculed Slocum's Easterners as "kid glove and paper collar" soldiers. Slocum's troops had proved their courage at Chattanooga in November 1863, however, and played a major role in the campaign for Atlanta.

When Sherman's men entered the city, they found it half destroyed, as this photograph shows (right). Union artillery caused much damage, but during their withdrawal, Hood's Confederates blew up warehouses, railroad depots, factories, and other important facilities in order to keep them out of Union hands.

THE PLAN TO MARCH

After withdrawing from Atlanta, Hood's army turned north to cut the single railroad that brought supplies to Sherman from Tennessee. Throughout September and October, Union and Confederate forces clashed north of Atlanta.

By November, tired of sparring with Hood, Sherman decided to forget about the railroad and get on with his next goal: the destruction of Georgia's resources. He ordered George Thomas and two Union corps to deal with Hood. Sherman and the remaining 62,000 men of his army would march through Georgia to Savannah on the Atlantic Coast.

It was a bold and risky plan. Sherman's army would be marching through the heart of the enemy's country, without a supply line and out of communication with the North. But the general was confident. "I can make Georgia howl," he wrote Union chief of staff Henry Halleck.

No troops would be left to occupy Atlanta. Sherman decided to evacuate the remaining civilians from the city and destroy anything of military value so that Atlanta could never again serve as a Confederate supply center. As Sherman prepared to leave Atlanta, his men began setting fire to the city. Sherman ordered that churches and homes be spared, but many of these burned as flames spread. By the morning of November 16, when the last of the Union troops marched out of the city, 200 acres of Atlanta lay in ashes.

Many historians consider William Tecumseh Sherman (1820–91; left) the first truly modern military commander. He was among the first to practice "total war"—the destruction of both an enemy's resources and its army. Sherman outlined his philosophy in a letter to Mayor James Calhoun, who protested the evacuation of civilians from Atlanta: "War is cruelty, and you cannot refine it . . . You might as well appeal against the thunderstorm as against these terrible hardships of war."

With flames from Atlanta lighting up the sky, Sherman's army began its march to the sea, as shown in this wood-engraving (below). They took only 2,500 light wagons of ammunition and medical supplies. As they marched, the men began to sing the popular Union song "John Brown's Body." An officer wrote, "Never before or since have I heard the chorus of 'Glory, Glory Hallelujah!' done with more spirit, or in better harmony of time and place."

SHERMAN'S MARCH

Sherman's men marched east, covering twelve miles a day. They faced little opposition. The only Southern troops left in Georgia were a few thousand militia (mostly boys and old men) and some cavalry commanded by General Joseph Wheeler. The Confederate militia tried to delay the Union troops on November 22, but they fled after losing 600 men in a brief, one-sided battle.

The Union Army was divided into two columns marching east in parallel lines. Between them lay sixty to eighty miles of fertile Georgia farmland, its barns and storehouses filled with a rich autumn harvest. The army turned this area into a smoking ruin, destroying crops, killing livestock, and burning houses.

According to Sherman's orders, "official" foraging parties were supposed to do the work of destruction, and private property was to be spared. Like Sheridan in the Shenandoah Valley, however, Sherman probably knew that his soldiers couldn't be controlled once the devastation began. "[We] destroyed all we could not eat . . . burned their cotton & gins, spilled their sorghum, burned & twisted their R. roads [railroads] and raised Hell generally," wrote one Union soldier to his family.

Even worse than Sherman's soldiers were the "bummers," groups of Union and Confederate deserters and civilian bandits who traveled on the fringes of the army, plundering homes and farms and sometimes murdering civilians.

This print (above), based on a painting by F.O.C. Darley, shows Sherman's men destroying Confederate resources. A slave family, freed by Sherman's approach, joins the Union column. A Georgia-born Union officer, defending Sherman's actions, wrote, "It is a terrible thing to consume and destroy the sustenance of several thousand people," but concluded that if the destruction convinced Southerners that their cause was lost, "it is mercy in the end."

Railroads were a special target of Sherman's army (right). "Let the destruction be so thorough that not a rail or a tie can be used again," ordered the general. To make sure of this, soldiers heated torn-up rails in bonfires and twisted them around trees—a technique the men called making "Sherman neckties" or "Jeff Davis hairpins."

"THE HIGHWAY FROM SLAVERY TO FREEDOM"

The two columns of Sherman's army came together at Milledgeville, Georgia, the halfway point between Atlanta and Savannah, and the "march to the sea" continued. When Union troops reached the town of Millen, they found the remains of a recently abandoned camp for Union prisoners. There was evidence that the soldiers held there had been starving and sick—including a mass grave with the sign "650 buried here." The men took out their anger on the surrounding countryside.

By now, about 25,000 newly freed slaves, including whole families, trailed behind the army. "Thousands of these poor people . . . trudged along, with no idea of where they were going, except they were on the highway from slavery to freedom," wrote a Union officer. Most dropped out as Sherman moved east, but about 7,000 blacks remained with the army when it reached the coast. Some were abandoned. When a Northern unit crossed Ebenezer Creek on a pontoon bridge, armed guards kept hundreds of blacks from crossing. Most tried to swim across. Some reached safety on the opposite bank, but many drowned or were captured by nearby Confederate cavalry and returned to slavery.

Hundreds of civilians, like the family shown here (right), fled their homes as Sherman approached. Sherman's troops encountered mostly women, children, and slaves on the march to the sea. In a letter to his wife, Ellen, Sherman described the "deep and bitter enmity" of Georgia's women towards the North: "No one who sees and hears them but must feel the intensity of their hate. Not a man is seen: nothing but women with houses plundered . . ."

In this wood-engraving (below), Union cavalrymen slaughter pigs and sheep. Sherman's cavalry (commanded by General Judson Kilpatrick, nicknamed "Kill Cavalry" for his recklessness) moved well ahead of the main body of the army. Being mounted, these troops could carry more plunder than the marching infantry.

THE BATTLE OF NASHVILLE

While Sherman marched to the sea, George Thomas's force, numbering about 60,000 men, faced 40,000 ill-equipped Confederates led by John Bell Hood. Despite the loss of Atlanta, Hood remained defiant. He decided to invade Union-held Kentucky and Tennessee, recruiting reinforcements for his Army of the Tennessee as he went. After defeating Thomas, Hood intended to march east to Virginia and link up with Robert E. Lee.

According to one historian, Hood's brash plan "seemed to have been scripted in never-never land." It started well. He managed to trap 30,000 Northerners under the command of John Schofield at Spring Hill, Tennessee, on November 29. Schofield's force slipped away under cover of darkness, but Hood caught up with the Northerners at Franklin late in the afternoon of November 30. Hood sent 18,000 men to charge the well-defended Union positions. The result was a slaughter: 6,000 Confederates, including thirteen generals, were killed, wounded, or captured. That night, Schofield brought his men into Nashville, where they joined Thomas and his 30,000 soldiers.

On December 15, Thomas moved out of Nashville in a brilliant attack that struck Hood's Army of the Tennessee on three sides. After two days of fighting, the survivors retreated south to Tupelo, Mississippi. In early January 1865, Hood himself asked to be relieved of command.

Thomas's men charge and capture a Confederate artillery battery during the Battle of Nashville in this Kurz & Allison lithograph (right). Thomas planned to strike Hood on December 10, but an ice storm held up the attack. Grant, unhappy at the delay, was on his way to Nashville to take over the operation when Thomas finally launched the assault.

Before beginning his drive into Tennessee, Hood tried to lure Union general George Thomas into a decisive battle by striking the Union-held railroad bridge at Altoona Pass on October 5. The Union commander telegraphed Atlanta for reinforcements, then told his men, "General Sherman says hold the fort!" The defenders, however, managed to drive off the Confederates before help arrived (below).

THE FALL OF SAVANNAH

While Thomas drove Hood south from Nashville, Sherman's men approached Savannah. On December 13, less than a month after leaving Atlanta, Sherman watched as his men captured Fort McAllister on the Ogeechee River just outside the city. Then a Union gunboat steamed into sight. Sherman's force, which Northern newspapers had dubbed "the Lost Army," was finally back in contact with the Union.

Less than 10,000 Confederate troops under William Hardee defended Savannah. P.G.T. Beauregard, in overall command of the city's defenses, decided that it was better to abandon Savannah than to lose any more men. He ordered Hardee to withdraw from the city, and on the night of December 20, the defenders slipped away. The next morning the first Union troops marched into the city.

Sherman missed the final moment of his march to the sea. The general was meeting with naval officers when his troops entered the city. Going ashore on December 22, he telegraphed a message to Lincoln: "I beg to present to you as a Christmas gift the city of Savannah, with 150 heavy guns and plenty of ammunition, also about 25,000 bales of cotton."

As 1864 ended, Sherman settled into the house of an English cotton merchant and planned his next move.

Hardee's Confederate troops entered Savannah by crossing the Savannah River on a hastily constructed pontoon bridge (above). They had a narrow escape. When the last Southern troops crossed just before 6:00 a.m. on December 21, the bridge was cut adrift. As he scrambled to safety on the river's north bank, Captain Robert Stiles, a Confederate engineer, saw the first of Sherman's men reach Savannah's waterfront.

Sherman offered the citizens of Savannah a chance to leave the city for other parts of the South. About 200 people, most of them relatives of Confederate soldiers, accepted the offer. Two Union vessels carried the refugees down the Savannah River, where they were transferred to Confederate steamships and taken to Charleston, South Carolina. William Waud, brother of A. R. Waud, sketched this scene (opposite, top).

In this wood-engraving from Harper's Weekly *(right), Southern civilians watch as Union troops enter Savannah. An important port, Savannah was spared the destruction that followed Atlanta's capture. Although there was some looting by Union troops, the city's 20,000 people got along reasonably well with the Union occupiers.*

THE FALL OF FORT FISHER

With Savannah captured, only one major port remained in Confederate hands—Wilmington, North Carolina. Wilmington was the last gap in the Union Navy's successful blockade of the South.

The key to Wilmington was Fort Fisher, at the mouth of the Cape Fear River. On December 23, a Union fleet carrying 6,500 troops prepared to attack Fort Fisher and shut off the Confederacy's last outlet to the sea.

The expedition's commander, General Benjamin Butler, had a unique plan. He anchored an old gunboat, the *Louisiana*, just offshore, and loaded it with gunpowder. Butler hoped that when the gunboat exploded, Fort Fisher would be blown sky high. The explosion, however, only created a spectacular waterspout. On December 24, the Union fleet began shelling the fort; by Christmas Day, the assault had already failed. Butler gave up and ordered the fleet home. Much to Grant's relief, Butler was finally removed from command.

Three weeks later, the Union resumed attack, this time with 8,000 soldiers under General Alfred Terry and a large fleet commanded by Admiral David Dixon Porter. On January 12, Porter's well-trained gunners began smashing the fort, while barges brought the infantry ashore to begin the land assault. At 10:00 p.m. on January 15, after four days of fighting, a patch of white appeared in the darkness. It was flag of surrender. Fort Fisher had fallen.

This wood-engraving (left) shows some of the damage caused by the 20,000 shells that hit Fort Fisher during the January expedition. Fewer than 800 Confederates defended the fort. Their commander, Major James Reilly, repeatedly appealed to General Braxton Bragg for reinforcements. Bragg finally sent 1,100 men, but only a handful arrived before the fort surrendered.

At one point in the assault, 2,000 sailors and marines—most of them untrained for land combat and armed with pistols and cutlasses—stormed Fort Fisher. As shown in this print (below), the Union troops broke through the fence protecting the northeast corner of the fort, but were driven back with heavy casualties. It was a gallant but unnecessary attack, as Union general Terry's infantry had already broken through at the fort's other end.

SHERMAN MARCHES NORTH

"Why, if Grant can keep Lee busy, we can tramp all over this Confederacy," wrote Ted Upson, a young soldier with Sherman in Savannah. The statement was close to Sherman's actual plan. He wanted to move north through the Carolinas, destroying their war-making resources as he had done in Georgia. Grant, however, wanted Sherman to bring his men to Virginia by ship for a major offensive against Lee. Sherman managed to persuade Grant that he could do more damage in the Carolinas than at Petersburg.

On February 1, Sherman and 60,000 men headed north from Savannah. For the soldiers, it was to be a very different experience from the march to the sea. Instead of clear, dry autumn weather, they faced cold winter rains that flooded the already swampy Carolina lowlands. Few obstacles had barred their route through Georgia, but the army now had to cross nine major rivers before they could reach their final destination—Goldsboro, North Carolina.

Sherman's army kept up a steady pace. Joseph Johnston, once again opposing Sherman, later wrote: "When I learned that Sherman's army was marching through the swamps, making its own corduroy [log] roads at the rate of a dozen miles a day, I made up my mind that there had been no such army in existence since the days of Julius Caesar."

On February 17, Confederate forces abandoned Charleston. The city had been under siege from Union gunboats and cannons since the spring of 1863. This photograph (above) shows the ruins of the Northeastern Railroad Depot in Charleston, one of the buildings destroyed in the long campaign against the "birthplace of secession."

As word of Sherman's approach reached Charleston, South Carolina, thousands of citizens fled the city, as shown in this engraving (right). They believed that the Union commander intended to destroy the city because the secession crisis that led to war had begun in Charleston a little less than four years earlier. But Sherman bypassed Charleston and took Columbia instead—where many of those who fled from Charleston had taken refuge.

SHERMAN'S ARMY IN THE CAROLINAS

The devastation caused by Sherman in South Carolina was worse than in Georgia. The earlier march, in a soldier's words, had been a "most gigantic pleasure excursion." They had plundered Georgia almost cheerfully, but in South Carolina a bitter desire for revenge took hold. It was this state's secession that had started the war. Now Sherman and his army would make the people pay. "Here is where treason began and, by God, here is where it shall end!" said one soldier.

Another described a typical incident of the march through South Carolina. After seizing a plantation, "the rich were put in the cabins of the Negroes; their cattle and corn were used for rations; their fences for . . . camp fires and their barns and cotton gins for bonfires."

The destruction ended when the army crossed into North Carolina on March 7. Because the state had wavered in its decision to secede, Sherman ordered that its people be treated "moderately and fairly." Once in North Carolina, Sherman met Joseph Johnston, who had scraped together 20,000 troops. Johnston was trying to head off Sherman before General John Schofield's force joined Sherman at Goldsboro. Johnston's force struck Sherman on March 16 at Averysboro and again on March 19 at Bentonville. Neither attack stopped Sherman for long. On March 21, Johnston withdrew to the west, and the 425-mile march was over.

On February 17—the same day that Charleston fell—Sherman captured Columbia, the capital of South Carolina. By the next morning, half the city lay in smoldering ruins (right). Southerners charged that Sherman had ordered the burning of the city. Sherman maintained that retreating Confederates had set the fires. Others blamed escaped Union prisoners or newly liberated slaves.

Realizing that a twelve-mile gap separated the two wings of Sherman's army, Johnston dug troops in along the road to Bentonville and attacked when the Northerners approached. Johnston's men kept them at bay until March 20, when Union reinforcements arrived (below) and drove off the Confederates.

PETERSBURG: THE BEGINNING OF THE END

By March 1865, the trench warfare at Petersburg, Virginia, was in its ninth month. Grant's line had slowly extended to cover more territory, forcing Lee to stretch his smaller force even farther to keep the Union trenches from completely surrounding the city. In some places, the Union and Confederate trenches were only separated by a few hundred feet. The men of both armies frequently called informal truces in order to talk and trade between the lines.

The war in Virginia had few major battles, but constant casualties from raiding parties, artillery fire, and sharpshooters were wearing down both armies. Grant did launch occasional attacks to strengthen his position. In August 1864, one offensive got within three miles of Richmond before being beaten back. In the same month, Union troops seized part of the Weldon Railroad, one of Lee's chief supply lines. In September, Union general Edward Ord's XVIII Corps captured Fort Harrison. For a moment, it seemed that the Army of the Potomac would make its long-awaited breakthrough, but the follow-up attack stalled and failed.

By the spring of 1865, Lee knew that his hungry, outnumbered troops could no longer hope to defeat Grant. In order to keep Confederate resistance alive, Lee needed to get his 55,000 men away from Petersburg and march them westward, where they could join forces with Joseph Johnston and his army.

Among the defenses used by both armies at Petersburg were chevaux-de-frise (right), which were movable lengths of sharpened stakes. Behind these outer defenses were zigzag rows of trenches, and behind these trenches were dugouts called "bombproofs," where men could shelter during artillery bombardments.

To deceive Union troops, the Confederates at Petersburg sometimes mounted logs on wheels and rolled them into the gun ports of their fortifications. From a distance, they looked like real cannons. Union soldiers dubbed them "Quaker guns" after the pacifist religious group. The Confederates in this print (below) have added to the trick by rigging up dummies to look like infantry.

FORT STEDMAN
TO FIVE FORKS

Lee hoped that an attack on Grant would loosen the Union lines and allow his army to escape. His target was Fort Stedman, just east of Petersburg. At 4:00 a.m. on March 25, Lee's troops stormed and captured the fort. Both Meade and Grant were away, and General John Parke found himself in command of the army with a major attack on his hands. Parke conducted a skillful defense, reinforcements arrived, and by 8:00 a.m. Fort Stedman was back in Union hands. Lee's last major gamble had failed.

Lee lost 5,000 men in the attack on Fort Stedman, stretching his already thin defensive line to the breaking point. The moment that Grant had so long awaited had finally arrived. On March 29, he sent a force to seize the road junction at Five Forks and block Lee's line of retreat westward.

Spring rains caused delays, and by the time Union cavalry under General Philip Sheridan reached Five Forks, 5,000 Confederates under General George Pickett held the crossroads. After Union infantry arrived, Sheridan attacked and drove off Pickett's men.

When Grant learned of the victory at Five Forks, he wasted no time in launching a major offensive up and down the lines around Petersburg. By the end of the day on April 2, the shattered Army of Northern Virginia was forced to retreat.

Union forces smashed through the Confederate earthworks around Petersburg on April 2 (above). A Union officer wrote that the Southerners were "swept away and scattered like chaff before a tornado" under the pressure of the Union assault. Among the day's casualties was the veteran Confederate commander A. P. Hill, killed by a Union patrol as he returned from a consultation with Lee and James Longstreet.

John Reekie took this photograph (right) of the first Union wagon train to enter the city of Petersburg shortly after dawn on April 3. In the ten-month campaign for the city, the Army of Northern Virginia and the Army of the Potomac suffered combined losses of 75,000 men—killed, wounded, or captured.

THE FALL OF RICHMOND

Jefferson Davis was attending the 11:00 a.m. service at St. Paul's Episcopal Church in Richmond when an aide brought him a telegram from Lee, reporting that the lines at Petersburg were breaking. The Confederate government had no choice but to leave Richmond.

The president hastily left the church to organize the evacuation. By nightfall, Davis, his cabinet, and what remained of the Confederate treasury and archives were rolling toward Danville, Virginia, on one of the last trains out of Richmond.

Some of Lee's retreating troops passed through Richmond in the afternoon, pausing just long enough to set fire to military stores in the city. As night fell, a mob made up of deserters, escaped convicts, and criminals burned and looted the city.

The first Union troops—black cavalrymen commanded by Charles Francis Adams, Jr.—arrived in Richmond early on the morning of April 3. A few hours later, President Lincoln, who had been visiting Grant at City Point, Virginia, arrived in the former Confederate capital, escorted only by Admiral David Porter and a few sailors. Most of the city's white residents stayed behind locked doors, but hundreds of newly freed slaves gathered around Lincoln, weeping and thanking him. "I know I am free," said one elderly woman, "for I have seen Father Abraham."

Black-clad women—perhaps in mourning for relatives killed fighting for the Confederacy—walk through a burned-out Richmond neighborhood in this haunting photograph (right). A Northern journalist wrote that in the fallen capital there was "no sound of life, but the silence of the tomb . . . We are under the shadow of ruins."

The carriages of Confederate officials stream across the James River as flames from the burning city light up the night sky in this Currier & Ives lithograph (below). A Southern reporter described the night of April 2 in Richmond: "Disorder, pillage, shouts, mad revelry of confusion . . . stores were entered at pleasure and emptied from top to bottom; yells of drunken men, shouts of roving pillagers, wild cries of distress filled the air and made the night hideous."

THE APPOMATTOX CAMPAIGN

The Army of Northern Virginia had lost a fifth of its force in the Union breakthrough at Petersburg. The weary, hungry survivors, split into five groups, now marched west toward Amelia Court House, a town about thirty-five miles from Petersburg.

There was supposed to be a supply of food at Amelia Court House, but when Lee and his men arrived they found only ammunition. They continued to march west on empty stomachs. Lee hoped to reach Danville or Lynchburg and eventually link up with Joseph Johnston and his army.

Grant was determined to stop Lee. While the Army of the Potomac's infantry pursued the retreating Southerners, Sheridan's cavalry raced ahead to block Lee's route. On April 6, the Union forces caught up with Lee's II Corps at Sayler's Creek. In a hard-fought but hopeless battle, the Northerners captured 6,000 men, including General Richard Ewell, and again split the Army of Northern Virginia.

Lee and the remnants of his army now moved toward Appomattox Court House, where two trainloads of food awaited the starving Southerners. On April 7, Sheridan's horsemen set out to capture Appomattox.

That night, Grant sent a message to Lee. It began, "The results of the last week must convince you of the hopelessness of further resistance." He asked Lee to surrender "that portion of the Confederate States Army known as the Army of Northern Virginia."

Surrounded by Southern wagons, wrecked and burning, soldiers of the Army of Northern Virginia's II Corps raise their downturned rifles in a gesture of surrender at Sayler's Creek (right). Those that didn't surrender immediately, wrote a Union private, "lost all formation and went across the country with our boys chasing up and gathering them in."

By the end of the Appomattox Campaign, Lee's men were surrounded on all sides by the Army of the Potomac, as this wood-engraving shows (below). Lee finally acknowledged his hopeless position, saying, "There is nothing left me but to go to see General Grant, and I had rather die a thousand deaths."

Description on back —

the last of Ewells Corps april 6

LEE'S SURRENDER

On April 8, Lee replied that he was willing to talk with Grant, but not to surrender his army, which continued to move toward Appomattox. That afternoon, Sheridan captured Appomattox Court House.

In the early morning of April 9—Palm Sunday—Lee's men made a final attempt to break out of the ever-tightening Union noose. The attack failed, finally convincing Lee that the end had come. He sent an officer to Grant asking for "a suspension of hostilities pending the adjustment of the terms of surrender of this army."

At 1:00 p.m., Lee arrived at the parlor of Wilmer Maclean's house in Appomattox, Virginia. Grant, his mud-stained outfit contrasting with Lee's gray full-dress uniform, arrived a few minutes later.

Grant offered generous terms. Lee's men would be allowed to return to their homes. Officers could keep their weapons, and soldiers who privately owned horses could keep them for use in their respective livelihoods. Lee agreed to all conditions, and at 3:00 p.m. the two commanders signed the surrender document.

As word of the surrender spread, Union soldiers began to cheer. Grant ordered them to stop. "The war is over," he said. "The rebels are our countrymen again."

Although this Currier & Ives lithograph shows them together, Lee and Grant actually sat at separate tables several feet apart during the surrender meeting. Hoping to make Lee comfortable, Grant began the encounter with small talk about their service in the pre-war army. Grant later wrote that he was "sad and depressed" when the moment of surrender came: "I felt like anything rather than rejoicing at the downfall of a foe who had fought so long and so valiantly."

THE END IN THE WEST

That night, the men of the Army of the Potomac poured into the camps of the Army of Northern Virginia to share their rations with the starving Southerners. By the next morning, news of the surrender reached the North. A 500-gun salute was fired in Washington. On Wall Street in New York City, "Men embraced and hugged each other . . . retreated into doorways to dry their eyes and came out again to flourish their hats and hurrah."

But the war wasn't quite over yet. Joseph Johnston still commanded almost 40,000 men in North Carolina. Jefferson Davis wanted to continue the fight, as a guerrilla war if necessary, but Johnston refused. "It would be the greatest of human crimes for us to continue the war," he told Davis on April 12. Five days later Sherman and Johnston met near Durham Station, North Carolina, to work out surrender terms. After tense negotiations, Johnston finally surrendered on April 26.

Scattered fighting continued in the West. The last battle of the war—a Confederate victory—was fought at the Palmitto Ranch in Texas on May 12 and 13. On May 26, General Edward Kirby Smith officially surrendered all Confederate forces west of the Mississippi. The Civil War was over.

At the war's end, Confederate soldiers who hadn't deserted and who had escaped capture or death still faced a strong enemy—hunger. Lee's army was barely surviving on green corn and apples until Grant ordered 25,000 rations be sent to Confederates following Appomattox. This wood-engraving (right) shows miserable Confederates grinding corn in the last days of the war.

This lithograph depicts Johnston surrendering his army (below). Sherman's original terms called for the Confederate states to be readmitted to the Union when their officials took an oath of loyalty to the United States. Furious that Sherman was meddling in political matters, Secretary of War Stanton ordered Sherman to offer Johnston the same terms that Grant had given Lee.

Resource Guide

Key to picture positions: (T) top, (C) center, (B) bottom; and in combinations: (TL) top left, (TR) top right, (BL) bottom left, (BR) bottom right, (RC) right center, (LC) left center.

Key to picture locations within the Library of Congress collections (and where available, photo negative numbers): P - Prints and Photographs Division; R - Rare Book Division; G - General Collections; MSS - Manuscript Division; G&M - Geography Division

PICTURES IN THIS VOLUME

2–3 army, P 4–5 flag, P 6–7 poster, P 8–9 map, G

Timeline: 10–11 TL, celebration, G; BL, Sherman, G; TR, poster, P 12–13 TL, Atlanta, G; TR, cartoon, P; BR, railroad, P, B8184-3631 14–15 BL, Petersburg, P, USZ62-15133; TR, Booth, P; BR, Appomattox, G

Part I: 16–17 Grant, P 18–19 TR, generals, G; BR, telegraphing, P, USZ61-805 20–21 TL, Banks, G; TR, map, G; BR, gunboats, G 22–23 TL, Forrest, P, USZ62-10724; BR, massacre, P, USZ62-33811 24–25 C, map, P, USZ62-65297; BR, battle, P, USZ62-12767 26–27 C, wounded, P, USZC4-1308; BR, battle, P ,USZ62-41630 28–29 TL, Grant on road, P, USZ62-7044; TR, battle, P; BR, map, G&M 30–31 C, battle, P; BR, Grant and Meade, P, B8171-730 32–33 C, battle, P, USZ62-12912 34–35 TR, battle, P, USZ62-7050; C, Hancock, P 36–37 TL, Semmes, P, USZ62-23312; C, boats, P 38–39 C, gunners, P 40–41 TL, Butler, P, B8172-1406; C, battle, P 42–43 TL, mining, G; TR, explosion, G 44–45 TL, Breckinridge, P, BH82101-5568; TR, Sigel, G; BR, mill, G 46–47 TL, Early, R; C, battle, P, USZ62-6872 48–49 TL,

Sheridan, P, BH825-43; C, battle, P 50–51 TR, Custer, P, USZ62-9225; C, Sheridan w/flag, P

Part II: 52–53 Farragut, P 54–55 C, battle, P 56–57 TL, *Tecumseh*, G; C, gunboats, G 58–59 TR, Cheatham, P, USZ62-91545; C, battle, P 60–61 TL, Hood, R; C, battle, P 62–63 TL, bridge, P, B8184-10107; TR, map, G&M; BR, battle, P 64–65 C, battle, P; BR, street scene, P, B816-8090 66–67 TL, Sherman, P, BH82-1979; C, march, G 68–69 C, destruction, P, USZ62-7333; BR, railroad, P, B8184-3630 70–71 TR, wagon, P, USZ62-33104; C, foraging party, G 72–73 TR, Nashville, P, USZ62-1289; C, Altoona Pass, P 74–75 TL, bridge, P, USZ62-31274; TR, boats, P; BR, Savannah, P, USZ62-31284 76–77 TL, ruins, G; C, battle, P 78–79 TL, ruins, P, B8171-3082; TR, evacuation, G 80–81 TR, ruins, P, B8184-10015; C, battle, G 82–83 TR, *chevaux-de-frise*, P, B8171-3215; C, dummies, P 84–85 C, battle, P, USZC4-1520; BR, wagon train, P 86–87 TR, ruins, P, B8171-905; C, fire, P 88–89 TR, surrender, P, USZ62-14654; C, surrounded, G 90–91 TR, surrender meeting, P 92–93 TR, Confederate soldiers, G; C, surrender meeting, P

SUGGESTED READING

BATTY, PETER AND PETER PARISH. *The Divided Union.* Topsfield, Mass.: Salem House, 1987.

CATTON, BRUCE. *The American Heritage Picture History of the Civil War.* New York: Bonanza Books, 1982.

FOMER, ERIC AND OLIVIA MAHONEY. *A House Divided.* Chicago: Chicago Historical Society, 1990.

SMITH, CARTER. *The Civil War.* New York: Facts on File, 1989.

TIME-LIFE. *Brother Against Brother.* New York: Prentice Hall, 1990.

Index

Page numbers in *italics* indicate illustrations

Adams, Charles Francis, 36, 37
Adams, Charles Francis, Jr., 86
Alabama (Confederate ship),
    36-37, *38-39*
Altoona Pass, 62
    battle of, *72-73*
Amelia Court House, 88
Appomattox Court House, 53, 88
Army of Northern Virginia, 18,
    30, 34, 40, 84, 92
    surrender of, 8, 88, *89*
Army of the Cumberland, 60
Army of the Potomac, 18, 28, 42,
    46, 82, *88-89*, 92
    casualties, 17
    Cold Harbor battle, *32-33*, 34,
        35
    generals, 18, *19*
    Wilderness battle, 24, *26-27*
Army of the Tennessee, 72
artillery, Union Army, 34, *35*
Atlanta, Georgia, 58, 60
    burning of, 66
    fall of, 53, *64-65*
    siege of, *62*, *63*
Averysboro, North Carolina, 80

Banks, Nathaniel Prentiss, *20*
battlefield promotions, 50
battles:
    Altoona Pass, *72-73*
    Bentonville, *80-81*
    Cedar Creek, *50-51*
    Cold Harbor, *32-33*, 34, *35*
    Fisher's Hill, 48
    Five Forks, 84
    Fort Pillow Massacre, 22, *23*
    Fort Stedman, 84
    Jonesboro, *60-61*
    Kenesaw Mountain, *58-59*
    Mobile Bay, *54-55*, *56-57*
    Nashville, 72, *73*
    New Market, 44
    Opequon Creek, *48-49*
    Palmitto Ranch, 92
    Petersburg, *40-41*, 42, *43*,
        84-85
    Sabine Crossroads, 20
    Sayler's Creek, 88, *89*
    Spotsylvania, 28, *29*, *30-31*
    Wilderness, *24-25*, *26-27*
Beauregard, P.G.T., 40, 74
Bentonville, battle of, *80-81*
blacks:
    soldiers, 22, *23*, 42, 86
    Union Army and, 70
    See also slaves, freed
Blair, Montgomery, 46
blockade of ports, 8, 53, 76
bombardment of Atlanta, 62, *63*
Bragg, Braxton, 77
Breckinridge, John C., 44

brevet officers, 50
British government, 36, 37
bummers, 68
burning of cities:
    Atlanta, 66
    Columbia, 80, *81*
    Richmond, *86-87*
Butler, Benjamin, 20, 40, 41, 76

Calhoun, James, 67
casualties, 17, 38
    Atlanta defense, 58, 60
    civilian, Sherman and, 62
    Cold Harbor battle, 34
    Franklin battle, 72
    Mobile Bay, 56
    Opequon Creek battle, 49
    Petersburg Campaign, 42, 84
    Spotsylvania Court House, 30
    Virginia Campaign, 82
    Virginia Military Institute
        cadets, 44
    Wilderness battle, 26
cavalry, 28, 48
Cedar Creek battle, *50-51*
Charleston siege, *78*, *79*
Chattahoochee River, 60
Cheatham, Benjamin, 58, *59*
chevaux-de-frise, 82, *83*
Civil War, 8, 17
    end of, 53
civilians, 44, 62, 70, *71*
    Charleston, *79*
    Atlanta, 66, 67
    Richmond, 86, *87*
    Savannah, 74, *75*
Cold Harbor battle, *32-33*, 34,
    35
Columbia, South Carolina, 78,
    80, *81*
commerce raiders, *36-37*, 38
Confederate Army, 17, 58
    casualties, 30, 49, 60, 84
    retreat from Savannah, 74
    See also Army of Northern
        Virginia; Army of the
        Tennessee
Confederate fleet, 54, 56
Confederate States, 8, *9*, 64
    and black soldiers, 22
    commerce raiders, *36-37*
    and fall of Richmond, *86-87*
crater, battle of, 42, *43*
Currier & Ives prints, *30-31*, *60-
    61*, *86-87*, *91*, *92-93*
Custer, George, 50, *51*

Dallas, Georgia, 62
Dalton, Georgia, 58
Danville, Virginia, 86
Darley, F.O.C., painting by,
    68-69

Davis, Jefferson, 53, 60, 64, 86,
    92
Democratic Party, 53
destruction:
    of Atlanta, 64, *65*, 66
    of Columbia, 80, *81*
    by Union forces, 17, 44, *45*,
        48, *66-67*, *68-69*, 80
Durham Station, North Carolina,
    92

Early, Jubal, 44, *46*, 47, 48, 50
economy, Southern, 53
XVIII Corps, Union Army, *33*, 82
Etowah River, *62*
Ewell, Richard, 24, 88

Farragut, David Glasgow, *52*, 53,
    54, 55, 56
Fisher's Hill, battle of, 48
Five Forks, battle of, 84
food supplies, 44
Forbes, Edwin S., sketch, *24-25*
Forrest, Nathan Bedford, 22, 23
Fort de Russy, 20, *21*
Fort Fisher, fall of, *76-77*
Fort Gaines, 54
Fort Harrison, 82
Fort McAllister, 74
Fort Morgan, 54, 56
Fort Pillow Massacre, 22, 23
Fort Powell, 54
Fort Stedman, battle of, 84
Fort Stevens, *46-47*
48th Pennsylvania Infantry, *42*
Franklin, Tennessee, battle, 72

generals, Union Army, *19*
Georgia, 8, 17, 18
    destruction of, *66-67*, *68-69*
Goldsboro, North Carolina, 78
Gordon, John B., 26, 27
Grant, Fred, 17
Grant, Ulysses S., 8, *16*, 17, 18,
    19, 32, 53, 58, 72, 88
    Cold Harbor battle, 34
    and Lee's surrender, 90, *91*
    and Mobile, 20
    Petersburg, 40, 41, 42, 82, 84
    Shenandoah Valley, 44, 48
    and Sheridan, 49
    and Sherman, 78
    Spotsylvania, 28, 30, *31*
    and Washington raid, 46
    Wilderness battle, 24

Halleck, Henry, 28, 66
Hancock, Winfield Scott, 26, 30,
    34-35
Hardee, William, 62, 74
Hartford (Union warship), 54,
    55, 56

Hill, A. P., 84
Holmes, Oliver Wendell, Jr., 47
Hood, John Bell, 60, 61, 62, 64, 66, 72
Hunter, David, 44

ironclad gunboats, 54, 56-57

James River, 40, 86-87
"John Brown's Body," 67
Johnson, Andrew, 6
Johnston, Joseph E., 58, 60, 62, 78, 80, 82
surrender of, 53, 92-93
Jonesboro, battle of, 60-61

Kearsarge (U.S. warship), 36-37, 38-39
Kell, John, 39
Kenesaw Mountain, 58-59
Kilpatrick, Judson, 70
Kinney, John, 54
Ku Klux Klan, 22
Kurz & Allison prints, 25, 73

Lee, Fitzhugh, 28
Lee, Robert E., 24, 28, 30, 32, 34, 40, 46, 50, 61
and fall of Richmond, 86
Fort Stedman attack, 84
Grant and, 17, 18
Petersburg siege, 82
surrender of, 53, 90, 91
Lincoln, Abraham, 6, 20, 46-47, 49, 62, 64, 74
assassination of, 53
and fall of Richmond, 86
Logan, John, 58-59
Longstreet, James, 26, 84
Louisiana (Union gunboat), 76
Lynchburg, Virginia, 44

Maclean, Wilmer, house of, 90
Macon & Western Railroad, 61, 62, 64
McPherson, James, 58
maps:
Atlanta siege, 63
Spotsylvania Court House, 29
United States, 8-9
Massaponax, Virginia, 30, 31
Meade, George Gordon, 18, 19, 24, 26, 28, 30, 31, 41, 42
merchant fleet, U.S., 36
Mexico, France and, 20
Milledgeville, Georgia, 70
Millen, Georgia, 70
Mobile, Alabama, 8, 20
Mobile Bay, battle of, 54-55, 56-57
monitors (warships), 56
Mule Shoe, battle of, 28

Napoleon III, Emperor, 20
Nashville, battle of, 72, 73
New Market, battle of, 44
North Carolina, Sherman and, 80

Northern states, 53, 64
Ogeechee River, 74
Opequon Creek battle, 48-49
Ord, Edward, 82
O'Sullivan, Timothy, photograph by, 31

Palmitto Ranch battle, 92
Parke, John, 84
Peachtree Creek, 60
Petersburg siege, 17, 40-41, 42, 43, 82-83, 84-85
Pickett, George, 84
political generals, 20, 41, 44
Porter, David Dixon, 76, 86
ports, Southern, 8, 54
Prang & Co. lithograph, 29
presidential election (1864), 6, 53, 62
prisoners:
Confederate, 28, 49, 88
end of exchanges, 22
Union, 70

Quaker guns, 82-83

railroads, 62, 66, 68-69, 82
Rapidan River, 18, 24
Rawlins, John A., 18, 19
Read, Thomas B., 50
Red River Campaign, 20, 21
Reekie, John, photograph, 85
refugees from Savannah, 74, 75
Reilly, James, 77
Republican Party, 6, 53
Richmond, Virginia, 82
fall of, 8, 53, 86-87

Sabine Crossroads battle, 20
Savannah, Georgia, 8, 74, 75
Sayler's Creek battle, 88, 89
Schofield, John, 61, 72, 80
II Corps, Confederate Army, 24, 88, 89
II Corps, Union Army, 34
Sedgwick, John, 28
Semmes, Raphael, 36, 37, 38
7th New York Heavy Artillery, 34, 35
Shenandoah (Confederate ship), 38
Shenandoah Valley Campaign, 17, 44, 45, 48, 50-51
Sheridan, Philip, 18, 28, 44, 48, 49, 50-51, 84, 88
Sherman, William Tecumseh, 8, 17, 18, 53, 58, 64, 66, 67
Atlanta siege, 62
Johnston's surrender, 92-93
march through Georgia, 66-67, 68-69, 70-71, 74, 75
northward march, 78, 80
Shreveport, Louisiana, 20
sieges:
Atlanta, 62, 63, 64-65
Charleston, 78, 79
Petersburg, 17, 40-41, 42, 43, 82-83, 84-85

Sigel, Franz, 44, 45
Silver Springs, Maryland, 46
Simsport, Louisiana, 20
VI Corps, Union Army, 32-33, 46
slaves, freed, 68-69, 70, 86
Slocum, Henry, 64
Smith, Edward Kirby, 92
soldiers, black, 22, 23, 42, 86
South Carolina, destruction in, 78, 80, 81
Spotsylvania Court House battle, 28, 29, 30-31
Spring Hill, Tennessee, 72
Stanton, Edwin, 92
Stiles, Robert, 74
strategies, 20
of Grant, 18, 58
of Lee, 28, 46
of Sherman, 78
Stuart, J.E.B., 28
surrender terms, 90, 92

Taylor, Richard, 20
Tecumseh (Union ironclad), 54, 56, 57
telegraph system, 18
Tennessee (Confederate ironclad), 54, 56-57
Terry, Alfred, 76, 77
Thomas, George, 60, 66, 72
total war, 67
tunnel, Petersburg, 42
Tupelo, Mississippi, 72
XX Corps, Union Army, 64-65

Union Army, 18, 19
black troops, 22, 23, 42, 86
casualties, 17, 26, 30, 34, 42, 58
See also Army of the Cumberland; Army of the Potomac
Union Navy, 8, 54-55, 76-77
Union Party, 6
Upson, Ted, 78
Upton, Emery, 28

Virginia Campaign, 8, 18, 82
Spotsylvania, 28, 29
Wilderness, 24-25, 26-27
Virginia Military Institute cadets, 44

Wallace, Lew, 46
Washington, D.C., raid on, 46
Waud, A. R., sketch by, 19, 26-27, 35
Waud, William, sketch by, 75
Weldon Railroad, 82
Wheeler, Joseph, 68
Wilderness battle, 24-25, 26-27
Wilmington, North Carolina, 8, 76
Winchester, Virginia, 49
Winslow, John, 37, 38
Wright, Rebecca, 48